THE ACCIDENTAL
ENTREPRENEUR

FROM CHILDHOOD MISFIT TO ENTREPRENEURIAL

SUCCESS

AN UNCONVENTIONAL BLUEPRINT FOR
TRANSFORMING YOUR PASSION INTO PROFIT

CHARLES HENRY THOMAS

AuthorHouse™
1663 Liberty Drive
Bloomington, IN 47403
www.authorhouse.com
Phone: 833-262-8899

Because of the dynamic nature of the Internet, any web addresses or links contained in this book may have changed
since publication and may no longer be valid. The views expressed in this work are solely those of the author and do
not necessarily reflect the views of the publisher, and the publisher hereby disclaims any responsibility for them.

Any people depicted in stock imagery provided by Getty Images are models,
and such images are being used for illustrative purposes only.
Certain stock imagery © Getty Images.

This book is printed on acid-free paper.

ISBN: 979-8-8230-2778-6 (sc)
ISBN: 979-8-8230-2779-3 (e)

Library of Congress Control Number: 2024912250

Print information available on the last page.

Published by AuthorHouse 07/18/2024

authorHOUSE®

TO ALL MY EXTENDED FAMILY.

PREFACE

This book is a compass for teenagers and young adults. Whether you're 13 to 19 or much older, the concepts and ideas here can steer you towards your true north. Who am I to offer this guidance? I'm an elder who has navigated a prosperous and fulfilling life. What holds true in my lifetime is still valid today but made even easier through the new and many applications of Artificial Intelligence.

As a young boy, I encountered many challenges mainly due to a lack of direction and guidance. My parents did their best, but like all of us, they had their limitations. Their eventual divorce when I was nine years old was a turning point for me. Rescued from a government boys' home by my grandmother and moving North to her home in Yorkshire.

A few years later, suffering from a teenage bout of severe delinquency, beaten up by none other than my school principal and making the decision to join the British Army at 15 years old. That was my escape from dead end streets.

Apart from my military experiences which holds 15 years of British Army life and learning, a larger proportion of this book references my journey through civilian life and various industries until connecting with Industrial Chemicals, initially as a self-employed agent and eventually running my own businesses.

Driven by a deep desire to help others navigate the challenges and opportunities of this current 2024 unsettled world I felt compelled to share my story and the lessons I've learned along the way.

Although this book presents my personal life journey, at the end of every chapter, there are paragraphs explaining why I took the actions I did, and the lessons learned from the experience. Many of which may be useful for you not only in your career but also in your interactions with other people; friends and strangers.

Many of those experiences and lessons will resonate with both young adults trying to decide their future career path, but also will be very useful for those who wish to make a career in sales.

This book is not a sales training manual, but it does show pointers and ideas that have been very successful for me and which I am happy to pass on. For me, sales were the opening to running my own business and you will discover in this book many ways and ideas to start a business of your own. Enjoy and prosper.

> *"A must read for anyone seeking direction, inspiration, and practical wisdom. This book is a treasure trove of insights that will help you chart your own path to success."*

David Willis, Deacon,
Saint Gabriel's Church,
Saint Louis, MO. USA

CHAPTER 1
TROUBLE AT MOOR

I was nine when the fabric of my family unraveled, leading me to the austere walls of a government-run boys' home. I spent four months there, homesick, bullied by the older boys and with little sympathy from the adult staff there other than comments like "You'll have to learn to grow up boy!" Thankfully, it wasn't long before my grandmother, Lillian Naylor, became my beacon of hope, offering me the opportunity to live with her after persuading the court that that would be a better outcome for me. We traveled by train to the mining heartland of Leeds, Yorkshire. Hunslet, our suburb, was a tapestry of soot-stained buildings and the relentless hum of industry.

My grandmother Lillian had lost her husband through illness several years before my rescue. I guess her offering me refuge was also a way to rescue herself from loneliness, although as you read on, you will notice that it was not a rescue from future heartbreak. Lillian was a kind, warm and loving mother surrogate for me. A great cook, seamstress, and housekeeper. In fact, everything was so much better than even my original life with my parents. Although we were poor, I did not want for anything living in Hunslet.

Enrollment into Hunslet Moor Secondary Modern School marked the beginning of my daily odyssey across the moor. The journey was a solitary mile, often shrouded in a thick cloak of fog and smog, a byproduct of the countless coal fires that were the lifeblood of our community. The winter months were particularly daunting; the smog became a tangible adversary, an almost living entity that I battled to reach the sanctuary of school.

Sometimes the pervasive scent of coal hung heavily in the air, a constant reminder of the town's life force. Yet, some homes bore the distinct, acrid tang of paraffin from the radiant heaters used as a frugal alternative. It was a smell that clung stubbornly to fabric and skin, a telltale sign of the lengths to which some people had to go to, to ward off the biting cold.

The early days at Hunslet Moor Secondary were a crucible of stress. My Scottish brogue (I was born in Scotland) was the brush that painted me as an outsider, inviting jests from my peers. But time is a subtle sculptor; it wasn't long before the Yorkshire lilt crept into my speech, and the taunts faded into memory.

Friendship, I learned, is often forged in the fires of adversity. The bonds I formed were with those who understood the gnawing pangs of poverty. Desperation was a shadow that trailed many of us, leading some down paths of rebellion. I found myself amidst a group of insurgents, challenging the status quo within school walls and beyond.

Yet, amidst the chaos, there was Carroll Wakefield—a beacon of common sense in our juvenile sea. Self-taught on the guitar, he could summon the spirit of Elvis Presley, his voice a conduit for 'The King' himself. Carroll's presence was a reminder that amidst chaos, there can be islands of extraordinary talent and wisdom. Carroll and I became best friends for life.

During those formative years with my grandmother, I was a tempest of youthful energy and restlessness. She tried to steer me right, but the call of mischief often overpowered her wise counsel. It was a time when my mind raced ahead without the brakes of foresight, leading me into a whirlwind of trouble.

I found camaraderie in the group that thrived on the thrill of dares. We were a band of young rebels, each challenge more ludicrous than the last, tempting fate without a thought for the consequences. It's a miracle that our antics didn't lead to serious harm.

Amidst this chaos, I faced a dare that would haunt me with guilt: to earn £10 before the weekend. In a moment of weakness, I betrayed the very person who had been my savior. I stole from my grandmother, the woman who had rescued me from the bleak existence of boys' homes and their harsh realities. The weight of this act of theft has pressed heavily on my conscience even now, a stark lesson in the price of dishonor.

Grandmother's home was a treasure trove of antiquity, her passion for collecting tangibles in every corner of the front room where she kept them. Pottery that whispered tales of ancient hands, swords that gleamed with silent histories, and chests that harbored the odd and mystical. It was from this collection that I, in a misguided attempt to meet a foolish dare, took items to sell. The shame of those actions lingers, a stain on the memory of my youth.

When the absence of her cherished items became clear, Grandmother was at a crossroads. The thought of involving the police was anathema to her and confronting me directly was a step she was not ready to take. Instead, she sought counsel from the one other authority in our lives—George A. Mathews, the principal of my school. It was a decision that would set the stage for a pivotal moment in my life.

The Confrontation

That Monday morning, the classroom's stillness shattered with my name, a summons to the headmaster's office that sank my heart. Mr. Mathews' office loomed like a lion's den, and there he sat, an imposing figure who seemed to embody the authority he wielded. His silence was a heavy cloak, suffocating the air between us before he spoke, his voice a low rumble of disappointment and accusation. "What have you done to your grandmother?" he asked, his words heavy with the weight of betrayal.

I stood there, a boy of excuses, claiming innocence where guilt lay thick. His rebuke was a physical force, his disappointment a deeper wound than the smacks that followed my feeble protests. The altercation escalated beyond words, leaving me bruised and bloodied, a stark reflection of the inner turmoil I had caused.

Sent home, marked by the encounter, I was a portrait of regret and shame. The journey back was a walk of introspection, each step a painful reminder of the trust I had broken and the path I needed to mend.

A Promise Made

Retreating to the solitude of my room, I let the silence of the house envelop me. The next morning, as I appeared, cleaned of the previous day's turmoil, I found my grandmother looking at me. Words were superfluous; our shared glance spoke volumes of the pain and understanding between us.

It was later, as she tended to my wounds, that the dam of my remorse broke. My apology spilled out, raw and sincere. Her response was not one of anger, but of grace. "I hope you have learned a lesson from all this," she said, her voice soft but firm. "Promise me it will never happen again."

With a heart swelling with gratitude, I made that promise wholeheartedly—a vow etched not just in words but in the very core of my being.

It is just what I needed!

I did not have a father to guide me. I had really stepped over the line, and if I had gotten away with it, I can guarantee that I would not have become the man I am today. I would have ended up in a prison like some of the boys I used to hang with. Why have I told you this very personal story? Well, my early childhood, even before I lived with my grandmother, was not good. I did not get into trouble, but my parents did, which is why I ended up in a boy's home. We lived in London at that time but my grandmother, Lillian, lived in Leeds, Yorkshire. About 196 miles away.

She is the one who pleaded with the authorities to allow her grandson to live with her and she managed to get me out of the boys' home, which was a truly horrible place. Today, there seems to be a growing situation where fathers are not present. The nuclear family as it was called, seems to be diminishing in society. With single mothers, divorced or not, bringing up children by themselves. Which is not conducive to a structured and healthy upbringing for a child, male or female.

Lessons Learned

Some of you may relate to this and others not so much. But my Headmaster, George Mathew's, beating me like that taught me a lesson and put me on the straight and narrow. It is simply what I needed at the time. Someone to knock some sense into me. Betraying the trust of my grandmother was the most shameful and regretful moment of my life. Betraying someone who has shown love for you and has faith in you cuts a deep wound in your life.

Dishonesty and deception, even over something that seems small like a youthful dare, creates a snowball effect of more lies and coverups that become hard to escape. Being dishonest may provide temporary satisfaction, but it comes at the price of guilt, damaged relationships, and losing people's faith in your character. Trust is the foundation of any meaningful connection - whether family, friends or in future professional settings. It takes years to build but can be shattered in an instant through thoughtless and unethical actions.

The disappointment I felt from my grandmother and headmaster compared to the pride and self-respect that comes from committing to strong moral principles like honesty and integrity is very tangible, you feel proud of yourself, of your achievements while doing something dishonest bring with it feelings of guilt and worthlessness which can make you angry at everyone including yourself. In the end it takes courage to do the right thing, even when facing pressure from some of your friends.

The path of deception is seductive but hollow. Real fulfillment comes from living with honesty and integrity, maintaining trust, and respecting those who love you." <u>Being able to like the person you see in the mirror is most important.</u>

From here, in the chapters to come, I will tell you what happened in my life and why things that I have learned may relate to you and perhaps place you in a better position to lead a successful life. I promise not to lecture you or tell you that you should do one thing or another, but I will try to explain as best I can why and how I did the things that turned my life into a success and may you learn from that.

I served a total of 18 years in the British Army. I reached the rank of Staff Seargent and was offered a QM's Commission should I extend my service to 22 years. but I had already decided near the end of my current term that I would close that era of my life. You see, I had never experienced adult working civilian life and I realized I would always be reporting to someone above me in the Military, I really wanted to make something of myself, perhaps even start my own business.

Throughout my life, post military, I have owned two industrial chemical businesses, a 50% share in a Telecommunications Least Cost Routing business that became the largest of it's kind in the UK, a 47ft motor yacht, a villa in Spain with two acres of vineyards and had the top cars of the time, BMW's and Mercedes Benz, cars of which I had owned several over the years.

How I achieved all that is part of the story in this book. I did not want this book to become a manual full of boring instructions but a story of how I lifted myself from failure to success even though I had a rough start in life like so many others in my time.

You might not have had a rough start to your life and therefore think that this book is not for you. You would be wrong! You want to be successful. You want the car, the girls, the boat, whatever your dreams of success mean to you. In this book you will get the basics of what you need to do to achieve your dreams and what to avoid.

Read on...

The crossroads of youth found me at Hunslet, where the echoes of industry and the whispers of ambition mingled. My school principal, Mr. George Mathews, a head teacher with a gaze that could cut through steel, saw potential in me that I had yet to see in myself. Over time we became friends, I was aware of his newfound interest in me since our fiery conflagration. His guidance was a compass pointing me away from the dead-end streets of my current associations.

Earning my keep by washing bottles in a chemist shop (drug store) on Dewsbury Road, I learned the value of honest work. The shillings I pocketed were more than currency; they were a declaration of independence, a rebellion against the expectations of my peers.

Yet, it was the arrival of Leonard, my grandmother's new companion, that truly tested my resolve. His attempts to assert authority over me were like flint striking steel, igniting a fire within that burned for autonomy. My emotions were all over the place. Leonard was like an intruder into the sanctuary of our home which, until he arrived, had settled into a very happy domain.

It was this, coupled with the desire to give my grandmother the freedom she so deserved, that solidified my decision to join the military—a decision that would soon lead me to the brink of mortality. However, my first brush was soon after the arrival of Leonard.

I wanted to go to see a movie one night, Leonard said to me, you must be back by ten pm or the door will be locked. By the time I had gone to my girlfriend's house to ask her if she would like to go with me (she could not, even though I said I would pay) and I had walked the mile and a half to the cinema, the main movie had already started.

In those days, the movies were run continuously. Short "B" movie at first, then Pathe News and cartoons like Tom & Jerry or Popeye the Sailor Man, followed by the main feature. The cinema would repeat that series of performances until midnight. Having missed a good 30 minutes of the main feature I decided to stay and watch the main feature again until I had caught up. By that time, it was 5 minutes to 11 in the evening.

That fateful night, as I ran home as fast as I could, the universe seemed to conspire to keep me from the confines of my bedroom. The cinematic escape I looked for had turned into a real-life drama, the kind that leaves a permanent imprint on one's soul. Being that late I had expected to be locked out.

A fire engine's ringing in the distance was an ominous harbinger. As I drew closer, the reality of the situation set in with a gut-wrenching clarity—the disaster had struck our house. The chimney stack had caught fire, collapsed and crashed through the roof into my bedroom. Landing on top of my bed, setting the room on fire from the hot fire bricks. In the aftermath, as we made makeshift beds in the living room, I couldn't help but feel a sense of surreal gratitude.

The arbitrary decision to stay at the cinema had unwittingly saved me from harm's way. It was a stark reminder of life's fragility and the unseen forces that sometimes guide our destiny. As I lay there, contemplating the day's events, I realized that it was a very lucky escape. Whether it was a guardian angel or mere chance, I knew that each moment of life was a gift not to be squandered.

I did not get much sleep that night. I began to think of all the clothing and personal things that had been destroyed by the fire. My guitar, the crystal set I had made several months earlier, my headphones Damn! The letters from my girlfriend had gone too! My clothing, what was I going to wear to school on Monday?

The master bedroom had not been touched other than the pungent smell of soot and smoke, but the firefighters had warned us the fire had weakened the floorboards of the passageway from outside my room to the bathroom and Grandmother's bedroom. We were somewhat hesitant to go up there, but Leonard suggested I go up and look, being as I was the lightest of the three of us.

When I climbed the stairs, I looked into my bedroom, it was as I imagined the night before. A complete mess, blackened by the smoke and flames, the ceiling had a big hole in it where the chimney had crashed through but amazingly the chest of drawers seemed to have survived being situated in the far corner of the bedroom.

The fire had destroyed my bed which had collapsed, burned and broken and the fire bricks had fallen onto the floor and spilled out into the hallway, burning some of the carpet and floor there. I gingerly walked over the burned area in the hallway to get to my grandmother's room and found that it was OK. So, at least Granny and I still had some clothes to wear, although everything needed washing to get rid of the stink of soot and smoke.

I had to have clean clothes and to look smart I thought because I had plans to visit the local Military Recruitment Office the following week.

Another Dreadful Event.

Six weeks later, the roof and chimney had been repaired, my bedroom had been redecorated, and the carpet in my bedroom and the hall had been replaced. Things were back to normal as much as they could be after that traumatic event. But there was another terrible event on the horizon that shocked my grandmother and me to the core.

One evening a few months later, Leonard was chastising me for something (I can't even remember what it was for), and he ended up striking me across the face. I retreated to my bedroom angry and resentful at the altercation and remember cursing him because of my anger and hatred for his intrusion on what was a comparatively happy existence before he arrived. The following morning, my grandmother's screaming awakened me, and I quickly got out of bed and ran to her bedroom.

I was stunned by what I saw, Leonard was on his back in the bed, his eyes wide open and mouth agape. He was dead! Through tears and heartbreak, my grandmother told me he had got up about 4.30am, unable to sleep, and gone downstairs to make a cup of tea. When he returned about half an hour later with a fresh cup for granny, he lay back down, but a few minutes later my grandmother heard a strange noise coming from him.

She tried to wake him to no avail, then got out of bed and turned the main bedroom light on. She was desperately trying to wake him, when I ran into the bedroom, but his eyes were open, but he was not breathing. Even though I was 14 years old and had not experienced a death before, I knew he was dead.

I dialed 999, and an ambulance arrived about 5 minutes later, confirming that Leonard had passed. I didn't go to school that week as I spent most of the time consoling my grandmother, who was obviously distraught. A sad time indeed but, I carried a lot of guilt in my mind because of the night before his death. I had cursed him in my teenage anger. For many years after, I had terrible dreams linked to that event, a form of what the modern world calls PTSD.

I thought that my presence living with my grandmother was a hindrance to her living a full and happy life. My inexcusable theft, the problems at school I was having from mixing with the wrong group, I needed a purpose, and I thought the military would be the answer.

That summer, at the end of the school term during the summer holidays, I decided it was time to make my approach to the military recruitment office, about half a mile away on Dewsbury Road.

The Recruitment Office

The day I stepped into the military recruiting office at 14 ½ years old marked the beginning of a new chapter. Despite the first setbacks with the Royal Air Force and the Royal Navy, the Army opened its doors to me, albeit with a waiting period until I was fifteen years old.

My grandmother's consent was the key that unlocked this path, and her blessing was a beacon of encouragement. She wasn't happy about it at all saying that I was too young to go into the miliary. Signing up for a commitment that spanned nearly two decades was no small decision, but it was one I made with a clear vision of the future.

The first three years promised not just military training but an education and a trade—a foundation for the life I aspired to lead. The departure from Leeds General Station was a poignant farewell to my dear grandmother, the woman who had been my anchor in turbulent times. I felt empty and troubled as I watched my grandmother disappear into the distance as we left the station.

The journey to Aldershot was a solitary one, but it was filled with the silent companionship of my hopes, dreams and some trepidation. I would have no friends at my destination, everything would be different. I could not stifle the emptiness I felt in my stomach during that long journey.

When the train pulled into Aldershot station, and I was greeted by a uniformed figure, I knew that my life was about to change in ways I could only imagine. A mixture of fear and excitement encompassed me until I arrived at my destination. Buller Barracks, a place that would shape me, challenge me, and ultimately, contribute to the person I would become.

Boot Camp

Joining the Royal Army Service Corps was my first foray into a world of regimented discipline and unyielding structure. The first months were a crucible, testing both my resolve and my ability to adapt. Homesickness gnawed at me, and the relentless routine of early mornings and rigorous training made me question my decision.

Yet, as I stood on the parade ground, boots gleaming and uniform immaculate, I began to understand the value of this new life. The drill instructor's voice was not just a call to order but a lesson in the importance of precision and preparedness.

The transformation from civilian attire to fatigues symbolized a deeper change—a shedding of old habits and a step towards a shared identity. The two-mile runs, the weight of the Lee Enfield 303 rifle growing with each step, were more than physical challenges; they were metaphors for the burdens we would learn to bear together.

I quickly realized that in this world, my actions had consequences not just for myself but for my entire squad. A misaligned bed or a tardy arrival meant collective punishment, a stark reminder that unity and synchronicity were paramount. From pushups to cross-country runs, each repercussion was a lesson in the importance of unity and the collective responsibility we shared.

So, this was my start into military life. What did I learn? I quickly found out that if I were late for anything or my bed was out of alignment, I would not be the only one punished, but my whole squad would receive the same punishment. Which could be anything from 50 pushups to running the 2-mile cross-country course in full kit and, if you slacked off the pace significantly during the circuit, you would be made to do it again.

You learned very quickly to act as a team. In the barracks you had to ensure that your bed was made military style, sheets and blankets folded with all edges lined up to form a box. Your bedside locker was to be open for inspection with your towels and kit folded all the same size and the stacked edges in line vertically. All this every morning because you had to get ready, standing to attention at the foot of your bed, for the morning inspection.

Every bed had to be lined up to form a straight line and there were usually 12 to 15 beds each side. The floor had to be "bumpered" to a high gloss. The bumper being a heavy rectangular metal weight with a long wooden pole for the handle.

The bumper had a folded piece of an old blanket underneath that was used to polish by swinging the bumper back and forth across the floor and underneath everyone's bed and into every corner. We all took turns doing this.

A couple of boys would sweep the floor while two more would follow with the bumpers and polish the floor. More would line the beds up, while others cleaned the ablutions (the bathrooms, sinks, urinals, and toilets).

If there was so much as a scratch on the floor, a blanket out of place or a dull shine on the boots that you had spent all night polishing to a high gloss (spit & polish) then not only the unfortunate boy soldier who had not risen to the occasion would be punished, but the whole platoon or squad would suffer the same punishment.

This taught us two things. Discipline, and that laziness in any form was not to be tolerated. So, everyone mucked in. Helping those who were a bit slow, there were always a few. We aggressively encouraged those who were tired or too lazy to get up in the morning; to get out of bed early enough so we would have time to do all our chores. We would not want all to get punished because one or two couldn't get it together.

We helped each other make sure our uniforms were immaculate for when we were on parade. I once got into trouble during a parade inspection because I had a twisted boot lace! That caused my squad to run round the parade square holding our rifles up in the air with both hands (God forbid if you ever dropped a rifle) for at least two circuits.

So, let us just have a look at what this experience has led to in my life and why now I consider it to have been of great value. Perhaps something that you could use as part of your endeavor to succeed in the world. I have no intention of encouraging you to join the military. That is a big decision only you can make, and it depends on your circumstances, not least of which is what your parents want for you. It is an honorable profession, but it always comes with considerable commitment and risk.

Lessons Learned

One of the most important things you will need to overcome in your life will be lethargy. AKA laziness. We all have that trait. Some, never rise above it, never find the ability to overcome their lethargy to the detriment of their future life. If you do not conquer your laziness, you will never have the time or the energy to become a success in the life you envision for yourself, whatever form that means to you in your imagination. You will not make that extra effort to become the best at what you do and at what you can be.

Reading this book right now, you may not ever want to join the military and will never have to go through the so called "character building" Boot Camp basic training that I did. I wouldn't call you fortunate for having missed that experience. Maybe you have joined a Dojo and gained some discipline that way. One day you will have to take some responsibility for your actions or inactions.

Your parents might cajole you for being lazy, but you ignore them anyway. Help, if you really must, but never ever offer (you might get the job). You are busy playing a game on your phone while your mother is dusting, cleaning the house, making your bed. What is that! 'Me' make my bed!

Being lazy is a habit! A bad habit sure, but you can change it by creating a new good habit. It only takes a little effort and some determination. You can start by making your bed in the mornings (every *morning, **MIAH**) and offering to help your parents, mother or father, around the house or help in other ways with what needs to be done.*

*Perhaps something simple, such as taking the trash out onto the street. Make it <u>your job</u> and `**Make It a Habit**' and surprisingly quickly you will find it such a natural thing to do, you will not even notice that you're doing it. The benefit to you will not only produce good vibes from your parents, but it will help you immensely in your future career, whatever you choose to do.*

*Now, you're probably asking yourself, "How can taking the trash out improve my life?" **<u>You missed the point!</u>** It is not the taking of the trash out to the curb that is the most important thing here, it is the creation of a new, important, good habit. The good habits you create now in your life will create a better life for you in the future.*

Being on time for an appointment is also a habit you should acquire. In the military if you're not 15minutes early you are 15 minutes late, whatever appointment it may be. If you make it a habit to be early for appointments, you will be surprised at what benefits you will reap. For example, say you must meet your girlfriend outside the movie theatre, and you get there early. When she sees you there waiting for her, she will know that you really like her and that alone will make her happy.

Now, let us tackle discipline. Discipline and laziness are linked together with habit. It takes discipline to get up a little bit earlier every morning to make your bed. It takes the big "D" word to clean the sink of your toothpaste and splashes in the morning so that you leave a clean and more hygienic place available for whoever follows you into the bathroom. Just make it a habit and you will hardly notice yourself doing it, but it will reap tremendous rewards in your life, I promise you. These are just examples. They also apply for getting to work on time, finishing tasks you have been given and reaching targets.

Making something a habit also creates self-discipline. I remember as a child a packet of sweets (candies) would last a week or so. These days I've watched children and adults devour a large packet of sweets in a few hours. No wonder diabetes is rampaging through the population. Self-discipline is a way you can control excess gratification.

The benefits are great! You will gain respect from your parents, your peers, even from your boss and it will therefore reward you for the rest of your life because those two things are so important to your happiness, your self-respect and well-being, not to mention your success. That's because people will know that they can rely on you and that you will turn up to get the job done on time, whatever it may be. habits and discipline enable you to achieve your larger goals and dreams. They are foundational.

Let's take it just one small step further. You fall in love, you live with a girl, and you hope to marry her in the future. Do you think it will last if she discovers that you are a slob? Being married is a partnership that means you share the responsibilities of living together, you married a wife not a slave. Take the trash out!

Those that do not learn this lesson in life will not make the extra effort to succeed in anything. But fortunately, they are easy to recognize. They have a distinct "It will do" attitude to everything, and beware, they will want you to join them in their apathy.

Next, we will have a look at why I changed my career in the Military, the countries I have travelled to, and the lessons learned from the experience that also may help you, in the future.

CHAPTER 3
GRUHN'S CAFE

At the end of our three months training and after we had completed our Passing Out Parade we were assigned to different barracks. I went to Borden in Surrey where there was an R.A.S.C depot. And soon after, I had my first furlough (back in England we called it "leave"). I had about four weeks off and I decided to visit my mother who incidentally had written a letter to me just two weeks before I had joined the Army. So, I already had her address. She had never written to me when I was at school or in the years I lived with my grandmother.

The letter was a bit strange, the gist of it was that she had now remarried to a person called Jimmy (Thomas) and that they had a small Cafe in Warren Street, London called "Gruhn's Cafe". She also said, being aware that from the age of 15 I would have finished my schooling, if I would like to work for them. I would be welcome, and I should visit them sometime. They did not know that I had joined the military boy's service. How could they? They never stayed in regular contact with me or my grandmother.

Well, I turned up in full uniform. My mother initially didn't recognize me but when she eventually realized who I was she was shocked. We cuddled, she expressed her delight and introduced me to Jimmy. Jimmy was an interesting person. A classic London Cockney. So much so that when he spoke, I could barely understand him, his accent was so profound. A Cockney is a person who was born within the sound area of the Bow, Church Bells, of London.

He was a true-red-blooded "Cockney" Londoner. We got on all right. They had an apartment above the Cafe and fortunately there was an extra bedroom where I could stay for the duration of my leave. We all got to know each other over the four weeks that I stayed with them. The one thing I must thank Jimmy for was his talk to me about my choice of career.

He asked me why I had chosen the R.A.S.C. to which I replied, "I didn't really have a choice at the Recruitment Office, the soldiers there suggested that I would be well placed in the RASC, and I would be taught to drive some big military equipment." Jimmy responded to that by saying to me, "You know kid, anyone can drive! Once you learn to drive a vehicle you can generally get into anything and drive it. You should take advantage of your time in the Army and learn a real trade!"

I considered that and it made a lot of sense to me, so I asked him what he thought was a good trade to get into. He mentioned a couple of occupations like engineering, signals, nursing but then he paused for a minute and said "You know what? Why don't you get into catering?" "You see, whatever is happening in the world, people will always need food, it's a business that will never go out of fashion and something that you will be able to fall back on for the rest of your life and even after you leave the military.

I thought that was a good idea. I never had any intention of working for Jimmy or Linda but learning a trade was an idea that motivated me. So, at the end of my leave, when I returned to my base, I made an appointment with my company commander. I told him that I wanted a transfer to the Army Catering Corps where I could learn a trade. Something that I could fall back on when I eventually left the force.

I can't remember him trying to dissuade me, but a few weeks later I was back in Aldershot only this time at the Army Catering Corps headquarters at St Omer barracks. There was a school for the boys so that we could continue our education plus a whole building devoted to what they called the Apprentice Chefs Training College.

It was driven into us quite early on that we were to be known as Chefs and were not to use the word cook ever again in describing ourselves, our training or future careers. I thought that was a good beginning. And thus, I became a chef. I did not realize how important that title was until I reached the age of eighteen and was formally inducted into what we called Man's Service.

I did well at the ACC Catering College. It was run as a true military establishment with the opportunity to earn rank and thus work your way up the hierarchy. In addition, the basic training I had received at the RASC stood me in good stead for this new environment that I was in. But it was not all a bed of roses!

When you are young and gaining confidence and respect because you are doing well in your training and education, you can get a little full of yourself. I had been promoted a few times to lance corporal and later to full corporal by this time. But, one day, during chefs training, I got a little too full of myself. The trainers in the catering school were mostly civilians, highly experienced and qualified chefs, having worked in top restaurants, hotels and other mass catering establishments. All of them deeply knowledgeable. Most were in their 40s or 50s and had strong life experience, a few also having served in the forces during the 2nd world war.

I cannot remember the reason I was rude and arrogant, but I remember I stormed out of the kitchen classroom and returned to my billet. The next day, fortunately, was an education day for us so I did not have to return to the kitchen classroom. However, on the way to the education building one of our senior NCO's a man by rank and name of Seargent Simons, pulled me to one side and talked to me.

"Son" he said, "you need to apologize to Chef Edwards. You need to get down off your high horse and apologize, because you need him much more than he needs you!" Simons said a lot more but was constructive rather than destructive and I agreed that the situation had got to my head and that I would definitely say I was sorry for my actions the next time I was in his class.

A couple of days later I was back in his class and before we started (there were at least a dozen students in the class) I went up to him and apologized loud enough so that everyone could hear. That same Mr. Edwards and I became friends over time to the extent that he spent extra hours training me so that I could compete at the famous bi-annual Catering Exhibition, Hotel Olympia in London.

I came first in my category competing against other military chefs from the Royal Air Force and The Royal Navy and a whole host of civilian caterers from hotels and restaurants from all over the country, which was down to Chef Edwards and his extra training and guidance. I not only had received great training from him, but I had learned another life lesson. Do you know what it was?

Lessons Learned

Humility

Humility and the ability to apologize when you are in the wrong. I am sure that had I not apologized to Chef Edwards when I was in his class. He would not have spent the time to help me personally or even have enrolled me as a competitor in Hotel Olympia.

It's easy to lose your temper and lash out verbally at someone and sometimes even to those who are trying to help you. Ask yourself this: Is it better to swallow your pride and apologize rather than allow things to fester and get out of hand? Which, if you think about it, is a loss to all involved.

I have seen marriages and best friends split apart for the lack of an apology. Too proud to admit that they were wrong or too proud to go the extra mile to calm things down and get back on an even footing. It's such a shame because stubborn self-pride can be very destructive when taken to the extreme.

Back in England a famous soccer player had an argument with the head coach about his commitment to training. The head coach dropped him from the next soccer match as punishment for his apparent apathy (that 'lazy' word again). The player went on-line and called the coach out.

The coach then banned him from playing for the rest of the season. The player, still upset, refused to apologize. Right now, at the time of writing, he is still not playing soccer and is exercising and training by himself. Who is right and who is wrong is not material here. Because this confrontation seriously damaged the team. In this case the team is above all individuals just like in the military if one person lets the squad down the whole squad suffers.

The player's pride and ego has ramped up the whole situation so much that now it's practically impossible for him to ever play for this globally famous soccer team again. The largest soccer club in the world with dedicated fans worldwide. The player earns $450,000 PER WEEK! That's an expensive amount of pride. He will not obtain that amount of money from any other club in the UK or Europe other than perhaps the Saudi Arabian clubs.

The team coach has the power to suspend and decide who will or will not play in any soccer match in any league. At the very least he deserves respect. When young soccer players earn such incredible amounts of money so early in life, some, unfortunately, get a very inflated impression of themselves. I think that might be the case here. He could have continued his career for at least another five years with the club at that incredible weekly salary and probably, if he were even more successful on the field, could have tied up further contracted years with a raise.

Pride

There is pride in yourself, the way you look and groom yourself, the clothes you wear, how clean you are, do you smell good. That is all self-pride and is a good thing. But pride can get out of hand and ruin people's lives. Pride mixed with anger can even cause death. So, it's something you should learn to control particularly when you're angry. Understand this: An apology is NOT a surrender. Think of it as a tool to take the heat out of a volatile situation that seems to be getting out of hand. Keep your head under all circumstances and you will always come out unscathed.

Saying sorry to your girlfriend, your wife, your brother or sister, friend whoever is upset with you, will take the heat out of most situations, and you can talk things through later when things are calmer. I have known life-long friends fall-out over silly arguments over which neither party has <u>any control</u> over whatsoever.

That situation is so common it's crazy. I've seen mothers and daughters come to tears due to arguments over things like politics, who's right and who's wrong over which neither of them has any control. Think about it, if you can't control something then why should you argue or get upset about it much less get into a fight about it.

Near the end of my time at the Chefs college and military school I had been promoted to boy Seargent Major. I was on duty at the time, midweek in the evening, and I had to inspect the boy's barracks. Not a drill inspection, just a check on the well-being of the new trainees.

Smoking was not allowed in the barracks. But I, in my senior position had become a little arrogant and thought I was above these rules. So, I was seen by one of the senior staff to be walking about the barracks, smoking! The staff member, a regular service man, a Seargeant, placed me on report.

The next morning, I was in front of our commanding officer, Major Gibson, who busted me back down to corporal. Thats three positions lower in the rank from SM. That happened only a few weeks before I was due to exit the school and enter my first real, grown-up posting. At least I managed to keep the rank of Corporal when I reported to my new commanding officer at the Royal Artillery barracks in Woolwich I could have been demoted to Private.

Empathy

Some people think that humility is a weakness when in fact it is just the opposite. An apology can actually build trust and respect in relationships, not diminish them. Humility enables continuous learning and growth where arrogance closes you off to new knowledge or constructive feedback.

Empathy gets its development from humility. Haven't you often wondered how some people can respond to you as though they can actually read your mind? When you're sad, for instance, and your mother knows exactly what's wrong with you but after a brief chat you both end up laughing at your silliness. Empathy is not a gift it is a developmental skill that arises from humility and consideration of other people's perspectives. Something worth honing!

To conclude this section.

The qualities of humility, willingness to apologize, pride management, and empathy may seem counterintuitive in a world that often celebrates brazen confidence and uncompromising individuality. However, as I've learned through my own experiences and observations, these traits are essential for personal growth, forging strong relationships, and achieving long-term success.

Humility opens us up to new knowledge and constructive feedback, enabling continuous learning and improvement. Sincere apologies, when called for, show emotional maturity and can build trust and respect rather than diminish it. Managing pride, especially in the face of anger or conflict, prevents destructive behaviors that can sabotage our goals and relationships. And actively developing empathy allows us to connect with others on a deeper level, defuse tensions, and find common ground.

While it takes ongoing practice and self-awareness to embody these qualities consistently, the payoff is immense. By cultivating humility, apologizing when appropriate, keeping pride in check, and leading with empathy, we set ourselves up for richer relationships, more resilient careers, and a greater sense of inner peace. These lessons, hard-won through my own trials and triumphs, are ones I hope you'll take to heart as you navigate your own journey through life.

This was a totally different experience for me. Now I was amongst grown men, some of them were volunteer military, others were conscripted (National Service) most, a few years older than me at 18 and some a lot older. This was my first real exposure to a working brigade kitchen where there were about 15 to 18 cooks under a staff-Seargeant who was in charge.

However, with my training and confidence, plus I was sporting a corporal's rank, I was treated with respect and some curiosity by those who had discovered I had spent the three previous years at the Apprentice Chef College in Aldershot. Once that information was out, I became known as Corporal Chef. I spent nearly 12 months at Woolwich and have a few stories to tell but I will narrow it down to only one to remain in the essence of this book.

One Friday I was off duty and Jimmy, a friend who was usually on the same shift as me, came into my room and threw his car keys on my bed and said, "I'm off this weekend Charlie...Going home with my mate Steve, who lives not far from me in Cheltenham so we're going in his car there and back. You can use my car if you like. See yah on Monday. Bye!"

Well Jimmy wasn't aware that I did not at that time have a driving license and left before I could even speak because his friend Steve was outside impatiently gunning his Ford Anglia. The next morning, I got up early and went to our private car park which was a massive compound watched over by a civilian security guard.

I eventually found Jimmy's car, an ex-police car, a Wolsey, if I remember correctly. I climbed in and sat there for a while getting a feel for the controls. Eventually I started her up, managed to get the car into first gear and slowly moved out of the parking space. I knew I would need to reverse the car at some time, so I practiced reverse there, making lots of high revving engine noises and the grinding of gears. The Wolsey was not an automatic car. Automatics were very rare in the UK at that time.

The guard I saw now was beginning to get curious, so I put the car in gear and slowly made my way out of the parking compound before managing 4th gear. That morning, I drove, untutored, unlicensed and uninsured, all-around Woolwich on major and minor roads, honing my driving skills.

By lunchtime I parked the car outside of my barracks and went in to see if any of the guys had left for lunch yet. There were still some there, so I said "Hey, any of you boys want a lift to the mess hall?" from which there were several hands raised. "Well, I can take four, who's coming?" Four got up at once and followed me out to Jimmy's car.

After lunch, after finding we were all off-duty, we all decided that a trip to the coast would be a great idea and Southend was the nearest seaside town so off we went, three in the back seat and one next to me, in the passenger seat. None of them had an inkling that this was my first time behind the wheel of a car.

Well, off we went down to Southend, Through the Woolwich Tunnel onto the main roads and eventually onto the main highway. I was getting quite comfortable driving the car but was not paying too much attention to the speed I was driving or the speed limits of the highway we were on. So, naturally I attracted the attention of a real police car, who started following me.

If you could have heard or read what was going through my mind in those moments, you would have had to laugh. Many were expletives relating to bodily functions and others were very near to sheer panic. What if they ask me for my driver's license and insurance, I asked myself. Oh boy, I'm in deep trouble here!

I had the good sense to slow down and let the police car catch up to me, expecting to be pulled over and stopped. Amazingly, the police car just pulled alongside of me on the highway, with the police driver giving me an admonishing look and waving his hand up and down in the universal movement denoting "Slow the hell down!"

Which I did gratefully, expelling a long-held breath from my lungs in the process.

We made our way to Southend without further problems and had a great time there at the fair, reveling in the fresh sea air and the freedom away from the unit. The road back was uneventful, and we all enjoyed the afternoon out at Southend.

Lessons Learned

Looking back on my reckless driving adventures, I realize how easily things could have taken a disastrous turn. As young people, we often run with a sense of invincibility, feeling immune to consequences until faced with a stark reality check. It's a mindset that can lead us to make foolish decisions, prioritizing immediate gratification over long-term safety and success.

One of the key lessons I learned from this experience is the importance of respecting laws and regulations, even if you think you can "get away" with breaking them. Driving without a license wasn't just illegal; it was a serious abuse of the privilege and responsibility that comes with operating a vehicle. Every time I got behind the wheel, I was not only putting myself at risk but also endangering the lives of my passengers and other motorists on the road.

It's easy to get caught up in the moment, especially when you're around older, more experienced peers who seem to navigate the world with confidence. But it's crucial to remember that our own actions have consequences, and we are ultimately responsible for the choices we make. Just because something seems thrilling or convenient in the short term doesn't mean it's worth the potential long-term costs.

Looking back, I'm grateful that my unlicensed driving didn't result in any accidents or legal repercussions. But I also recognize that my luck could have easily run out at any moment. It was a hard lesson in the importance of delayed gratification and the need to make decisions based on sound judgment rather than impulse.

As I've grown older, I've come to appreciate the value of self-discipline and the wisdom of following established rules and guidelines. Taking shortcuts or engaging in risky behavior might provide a temporary rush, but it rarely leads to lasting success or fulfillment. True growth and achievements come from putting in the hard work, practicing patience, and respecting the boundaries that keep us and others safe.

If there's one message, I hope you take away from my story, it's this: Don't wait for a close call or a catastrophe to start making responsible choices. Embrace the power of foresight and make decisions that prioritize your long-term wellbeing and the safety of those around you. And if you do make a mistake, own up to it, learn from it, and use it as an opportunity to mature and course-correct.

Life is full of temptations and opportunities to cut corners, but the rewards of living with integrity and discipline are immeasurable. By cultivating sound judgment and resisting the allure of recklessness, you set yourself up for a future of genuine success and peace of mind. Trust me, it's a lesson worth learning sooner rather than later.

CHAPTER 5
THE JOURNEY TO SINGAPORE

Ever since I was a child and had seen the movie Lost Horizon Shangri-la (1937) with Ronald Colman and Frank Capras I became fascinated with Oriental people and their culture. The military is a great opportunity to see the world. So, with that in mind I made an appointment to see my new commanding officer of the Royal Artillery Barracks to volunteer for overseas duty. Particularly for S.E. Asia or the Far East. The meeting went well, and he said he would put in a request on my behalf for the posting.

A month later I was on my way after a short spell of embarkation leave, on a great ship called the T.T. (Troop Transporter) Oxfordshire, a massive troopship leaving from Southampton. The night before embarkation I, amongst several hundred other British Army soldiers of various rank and regiments, slept in dormitories at the side of the dock where the ship stood waiting to set sail in the morning to catch the tide at 6.30 am. We were to have breakfast on board, so we embarked from 4am onwards until all were aboard.

Imagine my excitement. On my way to a totally different country on an enormous ship. So many firsts for me in my young life. When we started to move away from the dockside most of us were up on the top deck watching the process of casting off and leaving the dockside. Some had family waving goodbye. Not me, I had already said my goodbyes to Linda (my mother) and Jim (the cockney stepfather).

We stopped at many countries and Islands on the way to Singapore, which was to be my penultimate destination. I didn't even know at that time what unit I was going to be posted to or where in Malaya or Singapore I would eventually end up. But the journey was captivating.

Gibraltar

Our first stop was at Gibraltar. Unfortunately, I could not get shore leave there because I was on duty. Someone always had to be on duty in the dormitory decks where everyone's kit was stowed. We all had a bunk or a hammock and when we were up on deck or dining in the mess hall, someone had to remain on duty to guard the soldier's equipment and personal belongings. However, I heard from the returning soldiers about the famous Gibraltar monkeys and how clever they were at their attempts to steal from you. Apparently, they would jump on your shoulders, slide down your shirt and try to steal anything in your pockets. Some of the guys lost hankies, coins, all sorts of stuff including a few wallets. Only to see the agile animals run off into the distance screaming and yelping with delight.

Malta. The George Cross Island

Our next port of call was Malta. I managed to get off the ship there for most of the day and discovered "The Gut" an area with lots of bars, shops and entertainment. Malta was a very picturesque place with their unusually shaped boats in the harbor called Dgħajsa or Luzzu (pronounced "Dejes" for both) and their beautiful houses. I enjoyed my short stay there.

It was strange getting off the ship after you had already acquired "Sea Legs." The ship underway is constantly moving in many different directions. Forward, of course, but at the same time you're going up and down in the swell and side to side. Eventually you get used to it and acquire your 'sea legs" but many were terribly sea-sick from the effect. Once you get back on solid ground on shore you get the strange feeling that you're still rocking. It feels like the ground is moving underneath you. It wears off after a while, but it is very strange while it lasts.

Cypress

The next stop was Cypress, but I was on duty the night before and decided not to take shore leave. So, I was unable to visit the shore towns or shops, but it was interesting to stay on board as there were movies and games available, but I was more interested in the ship and managed to be shown the engine room. If you think of a car engine and then magnify that to the size of a large two-story house, you get the idea of how big the ship's engine was.

Suez Canal

A few days later, we were slowly cruising down the Suez Canal into the Red Sea. That particular journey was fascinating. A strip of fertile land on either side of the ship followed by desert in the distance of both port and starboard sides. I saw a priest dressed in a black cassock, wearing a big wide brimmed black hat called a "Cappello Romano" on the back of a donkey, riding down a pathway travelling in the same direction as the ship. It was like something out of a child's picture book, incredible.

Port Said (Yemen)

Further, as we entered the Red Sea the shorelines receded until we got to Yemen where we docked at a place called Port Said, (pronounced "Port Side") in Aden. On the way to the dockside while still on the ship we were surrounded by what were called "Bum Boats" These were native people trying to sell you "stuff" from their boats. I don't remember anyone buying anything from them besides the fact that you had to lower your money down from the porthole and whether you would get anything in return was another matter altogether. This time I had the opportunity to take shore leave for the day and ventured, with some friends I had made on board the ship, into the port town of Aden.

While in Aden we hired a taxi, the driver saying he would take us to the original "King Solomon's Mines" How original they were I'm not sure, but the journey was very interesting if very bleak. On the way to our destination the taxi driver stopped at a town further inland where there was a busy open-air market. That was a real eye opener.

I watched as a local woman bought some meat from a vendor. I think the meat was lamb or goat. I couldn't really tell because the carcass was totally blanketed with black horse flies. For the woman to see the meat she was buying, the vendor had a large straw feathered fly swatter which he used to scare the flies away temporarily so the lady could see what she was buying, yuk!

King Solomon's Mines were boring so eventually we made our way back to the ship. My memory of that short stay, apart from the actual poverty of the area, was of that "fly market."

Sri Lanka

The next stop was Ceylon, which is now called "Sri Lanka," the original ancient name of the Island. Sri Lanka was interesting, much more civilized, but everyone seemed to want to sell me diamonds and watches etc. I'm quite sure the diamonds would have turned into glass by the time they were wrapped and passed into my hands, so I didn't offer to buy them. Other than that, the people were very friendly, and the island was steeped in history and rugged beauty.

The Storm

On our way to our next destination Singapore, we entered the Indian Ocean and had to negotiate an impressive force 7 storm. The decks were roped off, all the portholes and hatches were battened down, loose items of furniture were tied down and no one dreamed of going anywhere near the canteen.

Why? Because many were terribly sea-sick, the whole dormitory deck was swimming with puke. Soldiers were vomiting all over the place because of the rough movements of the ship. Down below, the walls, the floors, the ceiling, everything seemed to be moving and the smell of vomit was gagging me, so I decided to make my way to the upper deck and into the fresh air.

I was lucky because I have never been seasick, but had I stayed there, down below much longer, I'm sure I would have joined all of them in the puking party, but I had to get out. Once I got up to the top deck level, I managed to open the hatch to get outside. What I saw there was incredible.

Everything and everywhere where the deck was exposed to the elements, was roped off, crisscrossing the open decks, so if you were crazy enough to be outside during such a storm at least you had something to hang on to. I maneuvered my way to the starboard side and wrapped my arms around the ropes there to keep me in place and watched.

I was told that if you feel seasick get out in the fresh air and look at the horizon. That will give your brain something to lock on to and your sickness will subside. But there was no horizon to see, all you could see were great waves. It was fortunate that I wasn't wearing a hat because the wind was strong and filled with sea foam and moisture, and it wasn't long before I was soaked to the skin.

This big ship was being thrown about like a toy. One minute I was looking up at a giant wave 50 feet above me as the ship was in the trough of the wave, Next minute we were on the crest of the wave, and I was looking down into the trough which seemed like hundreds of feet below me. I stayed there for what must have been over an hour.

The sea had calmed down a little by then, so I untangled myself from the ropes and carefully made my way to the saloon area, which fortunately was only one level below. There I found a few other guys hanging onto the bolted down sofas and looking green, but not puking.

That's something I will always remember. It was exciting and fascinating at the same time. The raw power of the sea and the ability of the captain of the ship and the helmsman to keep the ship pointing in the right direction, into and across the waves while being flung about from crest to trough in that storm was the catalyst for me to buy my own boat one day in the future.

Lessons Learned

My journey on the troop ship, with its diverse cast of characters and exotic ports of call, was not just a physical voyage but a profound learning experience. One of the most valuable lessons I took away was the importance of choosing friends wisely. In the close quarters of the ship, it became clear that not everyone who seeks your companionship has your best interests at heart.

Some individuals, I learned, are like fair-weather friends. They're eager to be by your side during good times, when you have something to offer, but they're quick to abandon ship when the waters get rough. True friendship, I realized, is tested in the crucible of difficult situations. It's about loyalty, support, and being there for each other even when it's inconvenient or challenging.

The experience also taught me the value of discernment in relationships. First impressions can be deceiving, and it's essential to observe people's actions over time to really understand their character. It's a balancing act - being open and friendly while also protecting yourself from those who might have ulterior motives.

Throughout the journey, I was exposed to a kaleidoscope of different cultures and ways of life. Each port of call offered a new perspective, a chance to step outside my comfort zone and see the world through a different lens. From the bustling markets of Aden to the ancient history of Sri Lanka, these experiences broadened my horizons and taught me the importance of adaptability.

The storm we encountered in the Indian Ocean was another powerful teacher. Amidst the heaving waves and the rolling and diving actions of the ship, I gained a profound respect for the raw power of nature. It was a reminder of how small we are in the grand scheme of things and how important it is to be prepared for the unexpected. But it also showcased the incredible resilience of the human spirit - the way people can come together and endure even the most challenging circumstances.

Looking back, I realize that the true treasure of that journey wasn't the exotic destinations or the souvenirs I collected. It was the lessons I learned about myself, about relationships, and about the world. Travel has a way of stripping away the superficial and revealing the essence of things. It challenges us, changes us, and helps us grow in ways we never could have imagined.

To any young person reading this, my advice is to embrace the opportunities that come your way, even if they seem daunting at first. Be open to new experiences, but also be discerning about the company you keep. Stay true to your values, even if it means standing apart from the crowd. And always remember that the challenges you face, whether it's a rogue wave or a fair-weather friend, are opportunities for growth and self-discovery.

The journey of life, much like that troop ship, will take you to unexpected places. There will be storms and there will be calm seas. But if you navigate with wisdom, integrity, and an open heart, you'll find that every port of call has something valuable to teach you. Embrace the voyage, learn from it, and let it shape you into the person you're meant to be.

We arrived at Singapore early in the morning. Everyone was awake and had recovered from the storm. The sleeping decks had been cleaned up and those, including myself, who were getting off here, were packed and ready to disembark. It always amazes me the difference between imagination and reality. When we landed in Singapore, I saw a modern (for the time) metropolis. And that was in 1959. Now, in 2024 you would see the same metropolis only much larger with more skyscrapers, modern railways running super trains, taxis and all that combined with modern luxury hotels, restaurants and fast-food stores. I was back in Singapore quite recently and noted the growth and modernization.

In 1959 it was still ahead of itself in terms of buildings and commerce with many international hotels, banks and top-class restaurants. We disembarked the ship, and I said goodbye to the friends I had made during my journey. Some going on to Hong Kong others landing here in Singapore but going to different regiments peppered around the island or up country like me, travelling into Malaya.

I was the only one going to Ipoh, which was in the northern region of the country in the Malay state of Perak. I had my military warrant, which was also my train ticket, and I caught a taxi to the train station which wasn't that far away. Had I known I could have walked.

The trains were, of course, different but I was happy, getting on the correct train and going in the right direction. On the journey, out of the city and over the Causeway Bridge connecting Singapore to Malaya I noticed a significant change. The area was much more rural and now I saw the beginnings of what I had believed to be the jungle. Much later, during my tour, I was to find out what the jungle was really like.

Ipoh North Malaya

I arrived at Ipoh train station about 5 or 6 hours later after many stops on the way. I made my way out of the station and right outside the main entrance there was a military land rover. The soldier looked up and asked, "Are you Corporal Thomas?" and after I replied in the affirmative, he got hold of all the stuff I was carrying and threw it in the back. I got in next to him in the passenger's seat. And off we went to my new posting. On the way, we passed through the town of Ipoh. I exclaimed. "My God, what is that awful smell?"

 It smelled as though a dozen animals had died and been left to rot in the sun, the stink was everywhere throughout the town. The driver, whose name was Bill, smirked and said "Don't worry mate, you'll soon get used to that. The smell comes from a local fruit called 'Durian" it has a thick casing which they cut off and leave on the street and that's what causes the stink, I know it's putrid, but you get used to it after a while."

We eventually got to the Unit, quite a large camp as an ordnance field park, and I met the duty officer who showed me where the offices were and where I was to be billeted. He also directed me to the cookhouse where I could get something to eat, I had eaten nothing since breakfast and that was at 5 am on the ship, in Singapore.

The cookhouse was pretty small to feed over two hundred soldiers, but I didn't worry, I knew that I could cope with anything as long as I had the rations and the main cookhouse facilities. The sleeping accommodation though was different from anything I had experienced before.

We were under what's called an "Attap Basher" Which basically is a long rectangular slab of concrete for the floor, with bamboo canes holding up the roof, wall panels made of some kind of giant palm leaves trapped between a bamboo frame which only rose to ¾ of the way to the roof. Above that was the roof. Again, made from a bamboo frame but with straw and leaves forming a thick cover over our heads. Electric lights hanging all the way down the center of the "Basher" and off-white mosquito nets over every bed.

I guess the "Basher" was about 400ft long and about 30 to 40ft wide. Giving plenty of room for the beds. One end of the Bashir there was a separate section for showers and sinks for washing etc. and even a further section for the toilets. The temperature was hot and humid, so I was grateful for the fans overhead every 10 or 12 feet apart.

I discovered that we had a local servant who made up the beds in the mornings and at night covered the beds with mosquito nets. You had to learn how to get into a mossy-net as they were called by the soldiers who had been there for some time. The trick was to pull out a small opening near the head of the bed and crawl through, keeping the net against your body as much as you could to stop the mosquitoes from joining you under the net.

Sometimes it didn't work! Many a night I would lay there listening to the high-pitched whine of the female mossy, waiting for it to stop. Then I would be slapping myself all over trying to smash the little bugger. Often it didn't work, and, in the morning, you found swollen bumps where they had fed.

Some of the lads didn't even use a mossy-net, they slept naked with just a towel over their hips for modesty. It was always hot and humid there so I could see the attraction if only the mossy's' would stay away. Eventually I found the secret. It was to get a good suntan and after a while the daily anti-malarial tablets we took "Paludrin," plus your darker tanned and tougher skin would prevent them from using you as a moving restaurant.

A Sad Day!

Two weeks after my arrival in Ipoh, I received some devastating news by mail. The letter was from granny's new companion, Johnathan Weirr. He told me that Lillian had passed away after a severe asthma attack that had caused her heart to fail.

After we had the fire in my bedroom all those years ago, when granny heard the crash from the chimney collapse, I remember she told me how she rushed to the door, which led to the upstairs. When she opened the door, there was a down-rush of hot smoke and soot, which she inhaled in shock.

Ever since that time, she had suffered from asthma. Of course, I was aware of this. She always sounded throaty and breathless after that terrible day. The last time I had talked to her was a few days before I embarked on the troopship to Singapore.

In the letter, he asked if I was going to return in time for the funeral and he also said that he and his family had cleared the house and boxed everything up and what I wanted to do with all her belongings. I was so upset by this news. I was 6,500 miles (about 10460.74 km) away and I had lost the only woman in the world who had loved me and taken care of me from when I was 9 years old.

I asked for compassionate leave from my commanding officer, but my request was refused, because I had only just arrived at my posting and there was no one to take my place. They had already been vacant, an NCO to run the catering for two months. The CO was a bit upset at the situation also, but he persuaded me with the response that I would fly all that way home and when I got there what could I do? It had now been nearly two months since she had passed.

He even said, "You would be lucky if there were any of her belongings left!' after he had read the letter. He also noted that the letter was from granny's address and not his family's home address. Then he asked me, "How would you find him?" I saw the logic in that because the letter was several weeks old before I even received it. He did not know where I was other than I was in the Army and overseas. So, he had mailed the letter to my last known UK posting to be sent on from there.

In the end, I didn't respond to the letter. The council would have reclaimed the house and new tenants would have been installed by the time I got there. I felt like that was another stain on my life because I couldn't get there. I had let her down once again.

Danger: Flying Frogs

There was one other pest that you had to be aware of and avoid if possible. A bug which we called, the Flying Frog. I have no idea what their true insect name is but these large insects are known for their bulbous eyes resembling those of a frog, therefore their nickname "The Flying Frog," their size and body weight together with their comparatively small multiple wings led to difficulties in flight control.

They seemed to have difficulty in making avoidance turns in flight. Quite often one would find its way into the basher to rest, then suddenly take off again. This thing was so heavy and solid that if it hit you in full flight, you would feel it. No sting or bite, just a welt where it had collided with you. Fortunately, in flight, it sounded like a miniature helicopter which gave everyone a warning, to duck!

Chit-Chats

There are many strange and wonderful insects and reptiles that live near humans in Malaya. One type of lizard we always welcomed was the Chit Chat. They are small Geckoes that also lived in the Attap Bashers with us. They were always welcomed because their main choice of food is mosquitoes. The little lizards knew where there were humans there were mosquitoes.

When off duty and resting on my bed I would see them running along the bamboo poles, hunting their prey with their long sticky tongues darting out catching mosquitoes and swallowing them whole. Often making their chit chat sound from which we gave them their name. Occasionally one would misstep and fall from the ceiling to land on your bed. But you never bothered them, after all they were your friends, they ate the mosquitoes, and they were cute, funny little things.

Perak Temple Caves

One event I must tell you about was when four of us, off duty, decided to explore the famous Perak Temple Caves, not far from Ipoh town. The caves are massive but inside each cave are incredibly large golden Buddha's. In one cave there is a golden Buddha laying down full length by one wall of the cave called The Reclining Buddha. In another cave there is one sitting cross legged. Each of the caves seemed to have one massive golden Buddha. It was an incredible sight to see.

A live one

Then we reached the last cave. As we entered, we heard chanting and saw a crowd of Chinese people kneeling in front of a Chinese Buddhist Priest dressed in full regalia with a golden mask with a beaded and feathered headdress. He was dancing about and chanting loudly when he suddenly collapsed into a giant golden chair. As soon as he fell into the chair, he started fitting and shaking violently, then he suddenly became still. At this time the crowd in the temple started throwing money at his feet and leaving the temple. The ceremony was obviously over but we stayed where we were standing with our backs to the rocky wall on a rock shelf where we could watch what was happening.

After a short while the priest opened one eye then the other and saw that everyone had left but us. He got out of his chair and took off his mask and robes then started walking towards us. I thought, "Oh oh maybe we are in trouble here!" But imagine our surprise when he beckoned us down, took off the last of his robes revealing a Cambridge University T-shirt. and said in perfect English. 'Welcome guys, I hope you enjoyed the show!"

He invited us to drink tea with him and we followed him into a smaller cave room which did indeed have a small kitchen where he boiled water on a gas stove and made English tea for us together with fresh milk. He introduced himself and told us he had spent many years in England. in fact, he had a degree from Cambridge University. We were all agape at the contrast.

One of us asked him why he was working there as a priest when he was so qualified and educated. He explained "Well first, I didn't like the weather in England plus, it was difficult for me to find a job there either as an interpreter or a priest. There are not many Buddhist Temples in the UK. So, my father, who is also a Priest, asked me to return home and practice the priesthood alongside him. Besides, as you saw, the money is quite good," as he pointed to all the Malayan Ringgits laying on the floor." We all laughed and thanked him for his hospitality. All of us loaded with a tale to tell of the famous caves of Ipoh.

Tanjong Rambutan, Ipoh.

Eventually I ended up in the Sergeants Mess and discovered I had two civilian cooks to help me, a Chinese cook a Malay cook and an Indian female cleaner. Now was the time I started work. This was my domain. Ordering food stores, making menus and learning the language. I realized that if I was going to earn the respect of the native workers, and, as I was going to be there (I thought) for at least three years I had better make the effort.

Things went well for me at the sergeant's mess, I completely changed the way food was presented in the mess and turned it into more of a restaurant atmosphere with menus at each table that the NCO's could order from. After a while some of them would come into the kitchen and congratulate me on the high standards and the changes.

It soon came to the notice of the Commanding Officer and other commissioned officers that the senior NCOs were getting better food and better service than they were. But they couldn't move me from the NCO's mess as the officers' mess only had a single civilian cook, so they really didn't have the excuse to move me.

Singing Sirens.

One day I was sitting outside the SGT's mess hall which was situated on a small hill looking down into the campgrounds. In the middle of the camp was an area about the size of a soccer field. Initially the idea was for it to be used for sports and exercise, but it turned out that more often than not when the soldiers were off duty they preferred to go into town and explore the delights of Ipoh.

While I was sitting there, I notice two women wearing black clothes covering them from head to toe. The hood not just covering the head but surrounding the face was like a tube, also black. Even their hands were covered, not by gloves, but by extra length in the arms and fastened somehow to keep the hands covered.

Both girls were wielding large scythes, spinning them around their heads and expertly scything the grass as good as any mowing machine. An incredible surreal sight. I learned later that many Malayans, especially the Chinese, were very careful to maintain their pale skin color and that was the reason they dressed like that.

What was even more fascinating was the music that was emanating from their mouths. Actually, they were calling and talking to each other but the sing-song sound of the Chinese dialect they were speaking was like flute music in a breeze delicately caressing your ears. The whole scene was hypnotic.

If I had a cell-phone camera like we have today and recorded a video of the event it would have hypnotized everyone that viewed it, I'm sure. Later, I approached them with cold water to drink which they accepted gratefully. That's when I realized they were girls, probably around 17 or 18 years old. I had not learned Malay or Chinese at that time so I couldn't communicate with them other than by signing and pointing to the water. It's a picture that has stuck in my mind ever since.

The Move to Malacca.

Less than a year later, the military camp in Ipoh was shut down and we moved to 28 Brigade Commonwealth International Camp in Terendak about 5 miles from Malacca Town. There, I was to take over the Brigade Officers mess catering. There were about 150 senior Officers spread across the combined Commonwealth Military Camp. From Generals, Brigadiers, Colonels Majors and on. Plus, on some occasions I had to cater for Royal guests. Mostly from Malaya but once from the UK and politicians from Australia, New Zealand and on one occasion a senior member from Nepal. Northern India representing the Gurka' regiment who were also at the enormous camp.

I was only 20 years old when I took on this responsibility, about 6 months after my arrival there, it was my 21st birthday. I remember that I managed to finish early that day as Chia, the beautiful Indian girl who had followed us down from Ipoh to Malacca. Said for me to rest as she would clean up and get everything organized for me so that the next day's breakfast would be ready for me to start.

I was surprised when Yusoff the number one boy (he was about 30 years old but that was his title). Knocked on my door and asked me to get dressed and follow him as someone of importance wanted to speak to me. He was very vague but insisted that I hurry. So, I got dressed in a traditional Sarong Kebaya and T shirt (I was off duty after all) and followed him towards the back of the Officers mess.

Imagine my surprise when I saw all the civilian staff, including the beautiful Chia, standing in front of a banquet of curries, rice, several different fruit, and drinks all laid out on four six-foot folding tables. Plus, a big birthday cake. When and where on earth had they cooked that, I had no idea! Well,

I was so very touched by their friendship and generosity. It was amazing. It was the best 21st birthday present I could have wished for.

I believe that a lot of it was because I took the time to learn the language, I still speak Malaysian now but like muscles if you don't use it, you lose it, and I am certainly not as fluent as I used to be. I always treated the civilian staff with respect, and many became close friends including Yusoff, Chia and Lee the civilian cook.

Lessons Learned

So many of my military compatriots' including surprisingly, some Senior Officers, tended to speak down to civilians even when they were off duty and in town. I always thought that was disgraceful. After all we were guests in their country not conquerors. Because I had taken the time to learn the language and befriend some of the locals. I was taken to fascinating places where no other soldier had been.

One place I was introduced to by some members of my staff was Tanjong Rambutan, where there is a big waterfall feeding fast rapids downstream. We would swim in the river there where the water was refreshingly cool. Following some of the native boys, I jumped from a ledge 60ft into the basin of the waterfall and got carried down the river with the current.

To stop myself from going too far, I grabbed an overhanging branch and at once was showered with loose twigs and branches. It was a few moments before I noticed that the twigs were all moving, trying to swim upstream. They were not twigs I realized but Stick Insects hundreds of them I had dislodged by grabbing the hanging branch to stop my motion downstream. Some of them were quite large.

Another time I was taken to a private swimming club. Such a beautiful place with a large kidney shaped pool with fountains and surrounded by great palm trees that kept the whole pool shaded from the sun. I was also invited to their houses for dinner which was a great honor that I took with humbleness and appreciation. I got a reputation with some of the officers staying in the mess, "Corporal Thomas had gone native!" Many, were jealous of my ability to communicate with the staff and that they had thrown a party for my 21st

My time in Singapore and Malaya taught me invaluable lessons about the importance of cultural sensitivity, respect, and the power of human connection. One of the most transformative experiences was learning the local language. By putting in the effort to understand and communicate with people in their native tongue, I discovered that language is a key that unlocks doors to friendship, trust, and cultural understanding.

Speaking the language allowed me to connect with my civilian staff on a deeper level, to appreciate their stories and perspectives, and to build genuine relationships based on mutual respect. It showed that I valued their culture and was willing to meet them halfway. The birthday celebration they organized for me was a touching testament to the bonds we had forged through our shared language and experiences.

Living in a foreign country also taught me the importance of cultural sensitivity and avoiding the trap of superiority. It's easy to fall into the mindset that our way of doing things is the "right" way, but that attitude only breeds resentment and division. I learned that true respect comes from approaching unfamiliar customs and beliefs with an open mind, a willingness to learn, and a humble recognition of our own limitations.

Through my friendships with locals, I discovered that despite our surface-level differences, we all share the same basic human desires. Whether we come from a bustling city or a rural village, whether we wear suits or sarongs, we all want the chance to build a good life, to provide for our loved ones, and to be treated with dignity. Recognizing our common humanity is the foundation for building bridges across cultures.

One of the greatest gifts of my time abroad was the opportunity to step outside my comfort zone and embrace new experiences. Swimming in the waterfalls of Tanjong Rambutan, exploring the temple caves, and immersing myself in the local way of life opened my eyes to the incredible diversity and beauty of the world. Each adventure brought with it a sense of wonder and a deeper appreciation for the richness of human experience.

My experiences in Malaya taught me that the true beauty of diversity lies in our willingness to celebrate it, to learn from it, and to let it expand our horizons. When we approach unfamiliar situations with humility and respect, we open ourselves up to the transformative power of human connection. And that, I believe, is the key to building a more understanding, more compassionate world.

I spent two very happy years in Malacca. I had a car that took me to town whenever I wanted to go. My car at that time was an MG TC, a black two-seater, that I used to race the 5 fairly straight miles to Malacca against taxi drivers who usually had Mercédès Benz diesel taxis and were always eager to race even when carrying a passenger.

Whenever you can visit or stay in a friendly country it is wise to make friends with the locals. I was lucky to have civilian staff at most of my overseas postings. Many became good friends. Should you visit a country that is not as advanced as your own, that is never an excuse to belittle and talk down to a native. Our birthplace is always happenstance, but I discovered that people are mostly the same as us. They all want the same things, a place to live, an education for their children, a happy life and a chance to lift themselves up from whatever financial level they are at.

My next posting was Hong Kong. I had served nearly three years in Malaya, but I was asked if I would prefer to have an added three-year tour of duty in Hong Kong or return to the UK. I jumped at the opportunity to extend my overseas duty as I didn't have anyone to go home to in the UK in my mind.

By sheer coincidence the very troopship I had sailed on to arrive in Singapore three years prior was now taking her final voyage as a military troopship and was going to stop at Hong Kong. So, I was lucky that my timing coincided with her final voyage, and I traveled to Hong Kong on the same ship.

When we arrived at Hong Kong it was early in the morning and very misty. Again, most of the soldiers who were fresh from the UK were all on the top deck looking at this new country we had been posted to. It was really a strange sight as we approached the dock with tugs helping the ship glide slowly into place at the dockside. Everywhere was shrouded in this ghostlike mist and we could only see the nearby buildings which were typical dockside structures.

We noticed that the steps had been opened by the side of the ship, but we had not been informed to disembark yet. So, we stayed where we were on the top deck and watched.

What I saw was like something from a movie or a comic book. What we saw were "Coolies." Chinese men and women wearing blue shorts and white shirts with their big "coolie" hats on, carrying stores up the stairs hanging alongside the ship and into the ship itself. This sight lasted about an hour before we were told to get ready to disembark. By Then the mist had disappeared and we got a good look at where we were.

We were docked at Kowloon which is not on Hong Kong Island but part of the Chinese mainland but still known as Hong Kong overall. Further inland you have an area called (at the time) The New Territories. All this land, Including Hong Kong, Kowloon and the New Territories was loaned to Britain by the Chinese Government under what was known as the 100-year lease.

Just before I disembarked, I received my orders and my promotion to Seargent. together with my final destination, which was a posting to The Royal Army Air Corps (not the RAF) which was situated in the New Territories at Fan Ling Gardens. The unit had a small airstrip situated in a valley surrounded by the Kow Loon Mountains.

"Kow" in Cantonese Chinese means Nine and Loon means Mountain so you can understand where the name comes from. The area of Canton in mainland China is a bit further north of Kow Loon so most people in Hong Kong originated from there and speak Cantonese.

Again, I was met by the driver of a military Land Rover who took me to the camp in Fan Ling. I was introduced to the Officer on Duty who directed me to the main cook house. There I got some refreshments and was shown to my room where I was to be billeted.After unpacking my kit and putting on my uniform I walked over to the main offices to officially report for duty to my new commanding officer.

The unit was quite small from what I had been used to, there were only about six or seven planes which were Auster's. Small single engine planes used for spotting, reconnaissance, mail delivery and the like. The pilots were all Officers, mostly Lieutenants and together with a support staff of aircraft engineers, signals and runway staff who looked after landing and take-off lights and signals plus kept the runway clear of debris. The total compliment being about 150 military personnel.

I had control of the main kitchen together with two civilians (Chinese) a cook and a cleaner helper. This posting was very nice for me. Situated in the middle of the mountains, away from the heat and the bustle of a very crowded Hong Kong and Kowloon, we had peace and quiet most of the time.

Two or three of the planes took off on assignments every day and the pilots let me know if they would be able to return in time for lunch or dinner. If they couldn't I would have a salad and sandwiches and maybe some soup put by for them for when they return.

Double Disaster!

A few months into this posting we had two disastrous episodes. We lost three pilots! To take off from the airstrip at Fan Ling it was necessary to run the plane to nearly the end of the runway, take-off, and as soon as you gain some height, circle to obtain more height sufficient to take you over the mountains. That was the best practice take-off situation.

At the end of the runway about ¾ of a mile in the distance was a low sloping start to one of the mountains and a couple of the pilots would occasionally run the planes up the side of the mountain at full throttle and practically skim the treetops to gain altitude to get over the mountain. I think between these two there were chicken bets on how many leaves they could knock off the trees on the way up.

One day they had an exercise which was ordered by central command. Three planes took off with the CO. The Adjutant, a Captain and the pilot, who will remain nameless, but was a two star Lieutenant. The Auster is only a two-seater plane but for some reason it was agreed by the three officers (all pilots) to remove the heavy radio equipment from the rear compartment which exposed a rear facing seat. That was where the CO was to sit.

With three people on board the pilot took off followed by the other two planes. I watched all this happening as the kitchens and small mess hall were near to the runway. The first plane took off and went for the mountain to climb it at full throttle while the other two planes peeled off and circled to gain height.

The first plane carrying the senior staff of our small unit, didn't make it and plowed into the side of the mountain. Everyone, including myself, shocked and horrified, ran to the mountain to see if we could help. We all climbed as quickly as we could through rocks and boulders surrounded by trees and overgrowth up the steep side of the mountain. Before we got to the crash site a helicopter was dropping medics and personnel near the crash site.

By the time we had scrambled up the side of the mountain the medics had already made their initial evaluation of the plane's occupants. The plane had plowed into the trees snapping the wings off the fuselage and the propeller and nose of the craft had buried itself into the soft earth and detritus of the surroundings.

The pilot and his passenger co- pilot to the right didn't make it, they were a bloody mess. The Major who was strapped into the rear facing seat faired only a little better, He was still alive when we got there but was unable to be moved. His back was broken, and he had other severe injuries. The medics decided that moving him would create more pain than he was in at the present. So, they stayed with him until his demise, which was a little over half an hour after we arrived.

In my opinion the deaths of these three officers were totally unnecessary and incredibly stupid. Had the pilot followed protocol they would still be alive today. Ego is the culprit here, and overconfidence that your control over the equipment you are using, in this case, the small plane, supersedes the capability of the machine itself.

Typhoon Wanda

In that part of the world there are fairly frequent monsoons. If you've never experienced a monsoon, it's like this, imagine someone tipping buckets of water over you onto your head. If you're driving, you have to stop because your windscreen wipers cannot cope with the down rush of water. You couldn't even call it rain because there are no droplets. It's like the heavens open and drop a small ocean on top of you. That is why in Malaysia and most tropical countries they don't have drains like we do in America or Europe. They have Monsoon Drains which are big enough to drive a car into.

A typhoon is a whole other animal. Think of a monsoon but with 90 mile an hour winds and you will get somewhere near to the picture. In 1962 Typhoon Wanda devastated Hong Kong and Kowloon right up to the New Territories including Fan Ling.

We lost the rest of our planes in that typhoon. Three of our ground crew were seriously injured trying to tie the planes down, inside their protective shelters when water flooded the area completely to a depth of about 4 to 5 feet depending upon the lay of the land. We were in a valley which didn't help much.

I spent some time in the kitchen before it got too bad, trying to salvage some of the stores. We didn't have windows in the mess or any of the buildings we just had shutters to keep off the rain, but Typhoon Wanda was too much and tore many of the shutters off their hinges.

I was just about to leave with a floating cart of salvaged supplies when something crashed into me from behind. I thought it was a table or something but when I recovered surfaced, and turned around to see what had hit me, I saw a Chinese man's body had struck me and was floating half on and half off our metal bain-marie, a serving counter.

There was nothing I could do for him as he was obviously dead and had been in the water for some time. My priority was to get these supplies out of the kitchen and somehow make my way to safety. I managed to get outside, but the wind was too strong, and tipped the cart I was pulling over, dumping everything into the water. I thought about going back inside to drag the Chinese guy out, but the water was getting deeper every minute, so I swam and paddled my way to the highest building on the camp which were the main offices.

There were about 15 to 20 men inside the building and when I entered, looking much like a half-drowned person coughing and spluttering water I had swallowed on the way to the offices. They all cheered that another one had made it to safety. We were stuck in the offices for a couple of hours before the typhoon stopped as suddenly as it began. When we ventured outside the scene was of utter devastation.

There were bodies floating around that had pooled near the cookhouse, and one of the officers ordered a group of us to grab the bodies and take them to high ground, lay them out and then to find something to cover them for families to identify later. Mostly they were civilians who had been working in the valley and had not escaped the deluge of water, rocks and uprooted trees pouring down from the mountain side.

Eventually nightfall came and we were still stuck in the offices. No lights, no drinking water, no electricity but we knew we would get rescued ourselves because we had got a message to RAF Kai Tak, and they said they would get to us ASAP. They had their own problems. Fortunately for us the radio control section was in the offices and had battery backup for just such an emergency.

It was daylight the following morning before we were rescued by the Airforce. They sent a couple of blue Airforce trucks for us. We had to wade through murky water for about 100 yards to get to the section of the road that was above water for the trucks to be able to pick us up.

We were taken to Kai Tak airport where we were temporarily billeted. I lost track of most of the guys as I was assigned to the Officers Mess, RAF Kai Tak for about three months while I waited for a new set of orders and a new posting. When they arrived, I discovered I was going back to S.E Asia to an Island called Labuan.

Labuan Island.

Labuan is a small island near the continent of Indonesia. To the north are the Philippines to the West is Brunei and Borneo both now part of Malaysia. Labuan lays just off the coast of Brunei. A stunningly beautiful Island.

My flight from Singapore to Labuan was a little hair-raising. There were four others taking the same flight, but we were all very surprised to see a Blackburn Beverly plane as our transport. I believe that all five of us expected a much smaller civilian plane for the 6 hour flight over the South China Sea.

The Blackburn Beverley was ideal for carrying large loads, landing on rough runways and dirt strips. It wasn't a particularly attractive plane, but it was apparently excellent for what it was built for, carrying heavy cargo.

One of our five members was slightly overweight, and I overheard a comment by one of his fellow travelers, "They must have known you were flying with us!" Cruel humor, but typical in the military. As the ranking member there, I just glared at the perpetrator but said nothing.

We all embarked through the only entrance we could see, the massive rear doors, and made our way forward to canvas seats set in the walls of the fuselage. The plane was empty apart from us. Soon after we were seated and strapped into our seats an R.A.F. lieutenant stepped down from the cockpit and made sure we were all ready for take-off.

The noise in the cargo hold was incredible as the plane quickly gained speed along the airstrip for what seemed a very short time and took off into the air. The journey was noisy and boring until about half an hour before our landing. The same lieutenant stepped down into the cargo hold with us again, only this time he had an urgent message.

The pilot needs you to all get out of your seats and move forward against the front bulkhead. Sit on the floor as close as possible and don't move. Because we're flying empty, we need to redistribute the weight as the fuel tanks get low.

So, we did as we were instructed and sat bunched together with worried looks on our faces. "Did he say we were running low on fuel?" I nodded in affirmation. 'Bloody Hell" he said, "what would happen if he had a full load, move tanks and land rovers forward to compensate?"

Upon landing with an uncomfortable bounce that jolted our buttocks, the realization dawned upon us: the pilot and the RAF officer had successfully played a clever trick on us. The joke was executed masterfully. With a jovial wave, the pilot bid farewell to us as we disembarked from the rear of the plane, strolled past the towering cockpit, and made our way to the quaint office near the airstrip.

Under Canvas

I discovered that I did not have to travel far in Labuan to my next posting. It was right next to the airstrip we had landed on. Yet another supply depot (an ordnance field park) of about 300 men including commissioned and non-commissioned officers. Everything, except the stores, the main offices and the mess hall, were under canvas. Usually, a 3-pole ridge tent could accommodate up to eight soldiers. The mess hall was an open sided attap basher like the ones in Ipoh that I had experienced before.

This time however, I had a separate building for the kitchen and one civilian Chinese who was born and raised in Labuan. To my delight everyone in Labuan spoke a dialect very close to Malay. So, I got on very well with Yuan our Chinese cook and helper. Yuan had been at the site for about six months before I arrived and was a very useful cook. He had worked at other British Army sites in Singapore before returning to his home in Labuan.

Lessons Learned

My experiences in Hong Kong and Labuan, particularly the devastating Typhoon Wanda and the tragic plane crash, taught me profound lessons about the fragility of life and the importance of living each day to the fullest. Facing mortality so closely, both through my own brush with death during the typhoon and the loss of my fellow officers, put things into sharp perspective. It made me realize that life is a precious gift, one that can be taken away in an instant.

In the aftermath of these tragedies, I grappled with nightmares and the weight of the memories. But through that struggle, I learned the value of resilience. I discovered that we have a choice in how we respond to adversity. We can either let it consume us, or we can find the strength to keep moving forward, to honor those we've lost by living our lives with purpose and gratitude.

One of the most important lessons I took away from this time was the need to fully engage with life. To embrace the laughter, the love, and the new experiences that come our way. It's easy to get caught up in the daily grind, to put off joy for some distant future. But my brush with death taught me that the future is never guaranteed. We have to make the most of every moment we're given.

Time is a fleeting resource, and it's up to us to spend it wisely. I learned that living with regret is a heavy burden to bear. When we face our own mortality, we often think about the things we wish we had done, the words we wish we had said. But we have the power to avoid those regrets by consciously choosing to live a full, meaningful life. By taking chances, expressing our feelings, and pursuing our passions.

The challenges I faced during this time, as painful as they were, also taught me about the transformative power of adversity. When we go through difficult times, we have an opportunity to grow, to become stronger and more adaptable. Each trial we face is a chance to learn something about ourselves, to develop new coping skills and perspectives that will serve us well in the future.

Throughout these ordeals, I also learned the value of human connection and support. The bonds I formed with my fellow soldiers and the local people I met were a source of comfort and strength. They reminded me that even in the darkest of times, we are not alone. That by leaning on each other and sharing our burdens, we can find the resilience to carry on.

Ultimately, the most important lesson I took away from this chapter of my life was the power of choice. We cannot always control what happens to us, but we can control how we respond. We can choose to live in fear and regret, or we can choose to embrace life with gratitude and determination. We can choose to let adversity define us, or we can choose to let it refine us.

My message is simple: life is short, and it is precious. Don't wait for tragedy to strike to start appreciating what you have. Embrace each day as a gift and make the most of every opportunity that comes your way. Face your challenges with resilience and lean on the support of those around you. And above all, choose to live a life that you can look back on with pride and satisfaction, knowing that you made the most of every moment.

Surprisingly, I managed to get significant time off even though we had three meals a day for 300 men. The last meal of the day was dinner, which was served at 5pm. For the guards we made individual sandwich packs for them as we had a guard hut by the main gate and where they could eat when they were not out on patrol. Also, there were always facilities for them to make hot tea or coffee to help them keep awake while on duty.

Not surprisingly the officers did not eat with the men. I only ever saw a duty officer enter the mess daily to check that everything was going OK. I found out that they ate at a small restaurant in town usually dining upon the local cuisine which was Satay (a dish consisting of small pieces of meat, grilled on a skewer and served with a spiced sauce containing peanut) which was usually a starter followed by a chicken curry Malaysian style.

Sometimes, I learned, by request the restaurant would provide something like an English meal, usually a steak or roast chicken and fries. The duty officers were always offered a meal with the men, or they could sit in my office. which most took advantage of gratefully enjoying the wider variety of British cuisine we had on offer.

One evening I was off duty, and together with some friends I had made at the camp, we went downtown to a small bar in the town, which was quite popular with off duty personnel, although this time there were only a few soldiers from the camp there. I had my guitar with me and sat quietly with my friends at the bar drinking Key Beer or Koonchi Beer as they called it over there.

Some of the soldiers were surrounding a very attractive local girl plying her with invitations and generally being pushy. The girl behind the bar saw my guitar and asked if I would play it. To which I agreed. Although she had heard me order drinks in Malay she would get a surprise at my next act.

At that time, across S.E. Asia, a Duch singer by the name of Anneki Grunlogh had made a big hit with a song in Malayan called "Burromb Cuko Lah." I had learned the song in Singapore and practiced it often on my guitar. When I played the guitar and sang it in Malay you can imagine the surprise of all the locals there.

All the bar staff and the Labuan locals in there, including the attractive young lady I had noticed, gathered round and sang the chorus with me, to the consternation of the soldiers who were trying hard to impress the local beauty. The soldiers were a mix of some from our ordnance camp and some flight crew members from the air strip we had landed on a few months back.

Back to the local beauty. She approached me, and speaking excellent English, asked how I could sing the local hit song. I told her that I had spent 3 years in Malaya and had learned the language from civilian staff that had worked with me. She became interested and we spoke both in Malay and English for the rest of the evening. In between calls for me to play the same tune repeatedly every time a local regular came into the bar.

Marina, and I, became good friends after that night and a few days later when I was off duty for the whole day, I hired a car and Marina who had invited me to spend the day with her, guided me to the most famous place on the Island called, Surrender Point (no pun intended). S.P holds historical significance even today as the site is where the Japanese Forces officially surrendered to the Australians on September 9th, 1945, at the end of World War II. (See Picture)

After visiting that historical site, we went to the beach nearby. What an incredible view of the sea and the sand. We changed into our bathing suits and left our towels and clothes on the sand as there was absolutely no one else in sight. The sea was warm and crystal clear. I had never experienced sea water looking so clear. As we paddled out into the ocean I looked down and could see sand crabs jostling away from our feet and fish darting in and around us as we pushed ourselves deeper into the water.

Imagine my surprise when we had waded over 150 yards out and yet the sea water was still only up to our waists. The sand dipped a little and the water quickly came up to our necks. We swam for a while, then kissed and held each other close before slowly walking back to the beach, Talk about an idyllic date. It was both romantic and breathtaking in the beauty of the surroundings and the beauty, warmth and passion of my date.

The Spy

One day, about six months into my tour of duty in Labuan, a friend and I discovered a small Kampong bar about half a mile from the camp. A Kampong is a small village made up of atap and bamboo dwellings usually mounted four or five feet off the ground to avoid the deluge of the monsoon rains they have during the monsoon season over there. Initially, we were there to barter for some fresh eggs and if possible, a few chickens that I would prepare and cook for the unit.

When we discovered the bar, we decided to see if they had any decent beers to drink which to our surprise they had. It appears that the black Irish stout seems to get everywhere. We sat quietly drinking our Guinness when I over-heard a Chinese person talking in Malay to a customer, asking very pointed questions about our unit.

He had assumed that the two soldiers dressed in fatigues were not conversant with the local language, which was a mistake. We were both armed at the time due to the emergency and it was requisite if you ventured outside of the camp boundary. We drank our stouts and waited outside for the individual to appear.

When he did, we at once cornered him, bound his hands and returned to our camp with him in tow. He offered no resistance at all and did not once open his mouth to protest. We reported the incident to our commanding officer and handed our prisoner over explaining the circumstances. The major called two guards, thanked us, and took charge of the prisoner.

We, complete with eggs, chickens and our weapons returned to the mess and began plucking the chickens (They had already been killed before they were sold to us) Yes sold, they didn't want to barter for anything we had but the price of the eggs and chickens in "Ringgit" the Malayan currency, was very acceptable so I paid and got reimbursed by our adjutant later.

Both my friend and I were called into the C. O's. tent and congratulated for being observant and understanding what was being said, with a glance at me. He told us the prisoner was being flown to Singapore where he would be further questioned and that we, were expressly told not to talk about it any further. And that was the last we ever heard about it.

During my time in Labuan there was some significant problems with the Chinese Military. Many had infiltrated down from the north through Thailand and passed the border land between **Kedah, Perak and Kelantan** at the northernmost area of Malaya. Due to this infiltration, all British military units in Malaya, which had now become Malaysia, were placed on high readiness.

At this time the guards on duty at our small unit by the side of the airstrip were issued with live ammunition for their rifles and Sten guns, (a small automatic weapon carried by some of the guards). I was off duty and lying down in my tent which I had assigned to me as the only occupant because of my rising before reveille to ensure that breakfast was available for everyone at 7.30 am.

The center post of the three that held the ridge tent up had an electric light suspended on a hook so I could clearly read my book at the time. Devastation occurred as I heard the center post explode and bullets whizzing around the tent above where I was laying. I heard shouting and deciding we were under attack I crawled on my belly together with dozens of other soldiers towards the armory.

We did not hear any further rounds being fired and we all made it to the armory safely. A duty officer was handing out weapons when the call came in to "Stand Down." One of the guards, a somewhat nervous fellow, had been surprised by an exaggerated shadow, probably from the perimeter lights, of someone on the side of a tent. Not thinking clearly and obviously frightened he emptied a whole Sten Gun magazine of 30 rounds into and around the camp lines!

Because the Sten Gun tends to rise under continuous fire and the soldier was obviously not trained well on the weapon, it saved anyone from being seriously injured. My tent was hit the worst, being closest to the mess but on the outskirts of the lines of tents and, closest to where the guard had fired. Once again, I was so lucky to have avoided injury because I had been laying down during the incident. That soldier was charged, Court Martialed and sent home to be later demobilized from the service.

I spent nearly a year in Labuan before I received new orders that I was to be posted to Germany for the next three years.

Lessons Learned

My time in Labuan confirmed the invaluable lesson of treating everyone with respect, regardless of rank, background, or nationality. Whether it was the locals at the bar, my fellow soldiers, or the potential spy we apprehended, each interaction reinforced the importance of seeing humanity in others. By learning the local language and immersing myself in the culture, I was able to build bridges, gather intelligence, and create meaningful connections that transcended barriers.

The night at the bar, when I performed a popular Malay song, was a testament to the power of music and shared experiences to unite people. The locals' enthusiastic response and the later friendship with Marina showed me that even amid military duties, there is always room for beauty, romance, and human connection. These moments of joy and levity are essential for keeping resilience and perspective in the face of the challenges and uncertainties of service life.

The incident with the potential spy underscored the importance of situational awareness and trusting one's instincts. By being attentive to my surroundings and picking up on subtle cues, I was able to identify a potential threat and protect our unit. This experience taught me the value of staying alert, thinking critically, and being proactive in the face of potential dangers.

The accidental shooting in the camp was a sobering reminder of the unpredictable nature of military life and the importance of proper training and discipline. While I was fortunate to escape unharmed, it reminded me once again of my escape from the chimney collapse in my childhood. Once again it underscored the fragility of life and the need for constant vigilance and preparedness. It also highlighted the profound impact that one person's actions can have on the safety and well-being of an entire community.

Saying goodbye to Labuan, and especially to Marina, was a bittersweet lesson in the transient nature of military postings. The emotional bonds formed during our time together made the parting all the more difficult. But it also taught me the importance of cherishing the moments and memories we gather in life, carrying them forward as a source of strength and inspiration in the face of new challenges.

Ultimately, my experience in Labuan reinforced the lesson that military service is a journey of constant adaptation, learning, and growth. Each posting brings its own unique set of challenges, opportunities, and life lessons. By approaching each new situation with an open mind, a respectful attitude, and a willingness to learn, we can navigate the complexities of military life and emerge stronger, wiser, and more resilient.

As I prepared to embark on my next chapter in Germany, I carried with me the lessons of Labuan - the power of human connection, the importance of situational awareness, the resilience of the human spirit, and the bittersweet nature of change. These lessons would continue to guide me through the challenges and adventures ahead, shaping me as a soldier, a leader, and a person.

Back to the future! Germany next and new adventures to follow.

Actually, Celle is a town not far from Hanover a major city in Germany. Where I was stationed was a little village about 4.5 miles north of Celle called Scheuen (pronounced Shoyne) The German Ordnance camp in Scheuen was not discovered until several years after the end of World War II. It was officially uncovered in the year 1953.

The German commandant at the time they were discovered was Herr Major Kurt Dostler. I arrived there many years later but there was still lots of history associated with this camp. A perimeter road ran around the camp with stores and billets, but the secrets of the camp, the main stores, were underground and were disclosed to us by a German named Otto Schmitz who had worked there.

I was placed in charge of the catering facilities for the whole camp. In addition, I was promoted to Staff- Seargent. The British commanding officer there at the time was a Major Peter Bird. He and I got on very well except for one event. Which happened in my 2nd year. I was quite proficient on the guitar in those days and wanted to form a group for entertainment during our off-duty hours.

Strangely there were no others stationed at the depot that could play an instrument so, I looked outside for civilian talent. By that time, I could speak a reasonable amount of German. In my search for talent, I visited a small nightclub off the main street in Celle and met up with a German guy about the same age as myself called Claus Ditmar. He played the guitar also and we teamed up.

Together we recruited a drummer and an accordion player. And eventually a military guy from another unit who played the saxophone. An eclectic mix to be sure. Clause was well connected in the area, and we initially played in pubs and dances around Celle. Shortly after we attracted the attention of the owner of the local nightclub, and we started playing regular gigs there.

We would play Beatles songs and Clause would sing. It was very amusing because although we played the music very well Clause could not speak any English at all, but he memorized and copied what he thought were the words. The chorus of the songs were easy for him like "She loves you, Yea-Yea-Yea" but the verses were something of a slur and mumbled effort.

Yet we were recognized and invited to play at the Star Club in Hamburg. The club owner in Celle took us there nearly every week late on Friday nights after we had finished playing in Celle, to play our new gig on Saturday evenings. The Star Club in Hamburg is quite famous for presenting the Beatles during their heyday and we ended up being the fill-ins for them. When they finished playing, we went on stage and did the intermediary stuff at which time most of the audience went to get drinks or pass water. It was fun, nevertheless. However, this caused a big problem for me.

With our increasing popularity we were asked to play more often and invited to play at other venues. We were bringing in more customers to the Celle nightclub. So, we ended up playing from 8pm until midnight Wednesday to Friday and then travelling after midnight on Fridays to Hamburg in the nightclub owner's car. For me it was becoming exhausting due to my military duties and working with the band.

I would get back to camp on Sundays early in the morning and before I caught up on my sleep, I made sure everything at the cookhouse was functioning OK. I had five well capable military cooks looking after things while I was out playing. Quite understandably that system could not be sustained. I got very tired of the constant pressure of my job as chef and the band work in the evenings and weekends. Things began to suffer!

Then, one day I was called in front of the commanding officer Major P. Bird, who, up until that time I'd had a very good relationship with. He informed me that he knew all about my gigs in Celle and my trips to Hamburg. He asked me about my intentions, whether I was going to continue like this or concentrate on my duties.

My response was I had become quite tired of the stress imposed on me from the late nights and weekends and that I was already thinking of dropping out of the band. I guess he liked that response. Because then he told me something quite surprising. "There are obviously two opportunities for you here, Charles" he said "One, I can have you out of the military within weeks and you could follow your career as a musician. Or, two, you can continue your military trajectory through to commissioned officer. For which I have already recommended you.

Well, I was stunned at that comment. I responded with "Are you serious sir?" to which he said "Why not? You have an excellent record, everywhere you have served you have left with a commendation on your records, and you have done an excellent job here. You are a qualified chef, and you meet all the educational requirements."

I didn't need to think too long about my response. So, with a firm "I'll finish with the band Sir!" I ended my brief sojourn with the band and that was the end of my musical career. I sold my guitar and have never picked up a guitar since. After my meeting with Major Bird, I had to really think about my future and what I wanted to do for the rest of my life. I was nearing the end of my commitment to the military and would spend the last six months in England.

There are so many stories I could tell you about my time in the military. Including the extra time on reserve I served a total of eighteen years. Whilst this book masquerades as an autobiography it's real intention is to highlight ways to succeed in life especially for young men and women who need a compass. Next comes the rest of my journey in civilian life.

Lessons Learned

You will Inevitably come to many crossroads in your life. My interview with the Major was one of mine. Once I had decided to proceed in the military, I never again took up an instrument to play music. The reason is simple. Had I done so I would probably have broken my word to the Major who was a bit like my Headmaster in Hunslet. Although he was my CO, he had become a friend and my respect for him ensured that I would do as I had promised.

That also got me to thinking about what I wanted to do with the rest of my life after my exit from the military. To be quite honest at that time I wasn't sure at all. I considered Mons Officer Cadets School, but it meant that I would have to sign the rest of my life away. I had several months left before my demobilization so I would come back to that conundrum many times before then.

Sometimes, if you're lucky, you have time to plot the course of your life before you are at a crossroads, other times you must make an instant decision. Instant decisions are the most difficult to master but during our lifetimes they come all too often and fast. Therefore, you must be ready with some idea of what you want out of life. So that when you have to make a major decision like that it at least conforms to what you want.

I'm not going to suggest it's easy because it isn't, but one thing I do know is that you can use your past experiences to help you make forward thinking decisions. But, here lies the problem if you have had a lot of bad experiences in your life it can restrict your view of the future for yourself. You must not hold onto a difficult memory or past other than to learn from it! If you do, sooner or later it will destroy you. The way I handle it is to compartmentalize.

You have a bad memory of an occurrence that haunts you or even a good one that you would rather forget so that you can carry on. Think of a trunk or a box of some sort and dump all those bad memories into the box, lock it and throw away the key! You cannot change the past you can only change the future. The bad parts you want to forget will come back to haunt you if you don't let them go.

It's metaphorical you say! Sure, it is, but it's a form of self-hypnosis that works. And it works on practically everything. Your memory holds all your life experiences good and bad. If you want to be a happy and interesting person lock those bad memories away. Just let the good memories flow.

You can do it. You see people around you that are so miserable, believing they have had a life full of bad luck and misfortune. They even seem to attract bad luck to themselves.

I never once believed that my unfortunate upbringing hindered me in any way in my life. It could have if I had let it! I have had an interesting and fulfilling life in the Military, and I enjoyed nearly every minute of it. When I think back now, I only think of the good times and smile. You do the same, think of the good times and smile. Throw the bad times away into that box and lock them up. My time in Celle, Germany, and the crossroads I faced with my military career and musical pursuits, taught me valuable lessons about decision-making, dealing with the past, and keeping a positive outlook on life.

One of the most important things I learned is the value of having a clear sense of purpose or a vision for your future. When you're faced with critical decisions, having a guiding principle or a long-term goal can help you navigate the choices before you. It doesn't mean you have to have every detail mapped out, but a general direction or aspiration can serve as a compass when you're at a crossroads.

Another key lesson is the importance of learning from your past experiences, both the good and the bad, without letting them define or limit your future. Every challenge and every triumph you've faced has shaped you and taught you something. It's essential to take those lessons and use them to inform your decisions and your growth, but not to let them dictate your path forward.

I need to repeat myself here because this is so important I'll put it in a different way. In dealing with difficult memories or experiences, I've found that compartmentalization can be a powerful coping mechanism. By mentally "locking away" the negative aspects of your past, you can prevent them from overshadowing your present and future. It's not about denying or forgetting what happened, but about choosing to focus on the positive and not letting the negative consume you.

This ties into the power of focusing on the good memories and experiences in your life. When you make a conscious effort to remember and cherish the positive moments, you attract more positivity into your life. It's like training your mind to look for the good, even in challenging situations. And when you radiate that positive energy, it has a ripple effect on those around you.

It's also crucial to recognize the role of personal responsibility in shaping your own narrative. Your past hardships or misfortunes do not have to define your future. You have the power to choose how you interpret and respond to the events of your life. By taking ownership of your story and your choices, you reclaim control over your destiny.

Integrity and keeping your word are also paramount, as shown in my commitment to Major Bird. When you make a promise or a decision, following through on it not only builds trust and respect with others but also reinforces your own sense of character and self-respect. It's about aligning your actions with your values and being true to yourself.

As I prepared to transition into civilian life, I realized that embracing the uncertainties of the future with a sense of curiosity and openness is key. While it's important to have goals and aspirations, life rarely follows a strict plan. Being adaptable, open to new opportunities, and willing to learn and grow as you go, will serve you well in any path you choose.

Ultimately, the lessons I learned in Celle, and throughout my military career, have shaped me into the person I am today. They've taught me resilience, integrity, and the power of a positive mindset. As I looked ahead to my civilian journey, I carried these lessons with me, knowing that they would guide me through whatever challenges and opportunities lay ahead.

My final Posting was to a Military Police unit based just outside Chester in the UK. Not a large base only about 250 men. I had three Army Catering Corps cooks with me and between us we looked after the catering for the unit. I thought this was going to be a boring 6 months but boy was I wrong!

The first surprise only a few weeks later was a 2-week exercise in the Grobbendonk countryside in Belgium. It was time to put my knowledge of field catering craft into action once again. The three ACC cooks and I loaded our field kitchen equipment onto our designated army truck making sure that our Number 1 burners and fuel were carefully secured away from the food supplies and utensils. The cooks rode with the stores on the back of the truck while I rode in a land rover with our personal gear and civvies (off duty civilian clothing).

We rode in convoy down to Dover and crossed the channel to Ostend. From there we continued on until we reached Grobbendonk. A pretty town surrounded by farmland and fields with a smattering of woodland. We set our equipment up and produced a pretty effective field kitchen. The number 1 burners sounded like jet engines once they were fired up.

The burner is a very simple but effective design. Basically a 5-gallon circular steel tank which is filled with petrol (gas) and pumped up to a high pressure. A valve on the side is opened and the fuel enters a vortex under pressure, which vaporizes the fuel. Once set alight it throws a roaring hot jet of fire that can be adjusted in length by a valve on the side. Imagine jet plane exhaust and you'll get the idea of how powerful these things were.

We dug two long trenches 3ft wide, 15 to 20ft long and covered the trenches with metal plates that had oval holes in them to fit the oval bottoms of our metal field buckets. These were used to produce tea, stew, vegetables, mash and a whole variety of food that we had brought with us. The cooking heat was controlled by moving the buckets close to the burner or farther away depending upon what was needed.

We served straight out of the buckets. It was a very successful system and we produced tasty and nourishing food for over 1000 men and women after all the various units had arrived. Strangely this was my first large scale experience of field cooking, and it happened so near the end of my military career. We were commended by the brigadier and some of his staff for how organized we were and the quality of the food we served during the exercise.

Before the exercise had finished, we managed to get some time off and visited Grobbendonk town. Two of the cooks, and an Infantry Seargent joined us as we ventured into the town square near the post office. There was a club that sold food and beer, so we entered that establishment in anticipation of sampling some excellent Belgium food and liquid refreshment. You can imagine our surprise when we realized we had entered a Belgium clip-joint! No sooner had we chosen a large booth and sat down when we were joined by a couple of scantily clad but very attractive women.

They both spoke fairly good if heavily accented English and took our order for drinks. A waiter returned with the drinks pretty quickly and deposited them in front of us. Of course there were drinks for the girls also. The time was midafternoon so there were very few people at the bar, probably most were at work. Well, the Seargent seemed to be very taken with one of the girls and their hands were touching across the table.

I thought "Wow that was quick!" but I was even further amazed as they both got up and walked towards the stairs leading up towards the second floor above. Not 10 minutes later he came running back down the stairs red-faced and cursing. We looked up and as we heard him approach our table. He shouted out. "SHE has a bigger dick than I have down there. It's a guy!" We just couldn't help it, we just rolled about laughing and made our way out of the club. The young Seargent cursed his disappointment and embarrassment. I asked him jokingly, "If SHE had a smaller dick than his would it have made a difference? Everyone laughed at that, but he just glared at me and mumbled something that sounded like "Smart Ass!"

My first venture into sales.

Back in Chester at the unit, with about five months left of my service to complete I began to think seriously about what I was going to do. I read somewhere that selling was a well-paying job if you're successful. That job required travelling and meeting potential clients to sell your products to. Sometimes you were supplied with a nice car and an expense account to help you travel to the customer's premises. I thought that was something I could do so I visited the local library to find any books I could on selling.

I discovered two books that I thought would help me. One was called "**How I raised myself from failure to success in selling" By Frank Bettger.** That was an extremely helpful book which I believed contributed significantly to my success. The other book I borrowed was, **"How to win friends and Influence People" by Dale Carnegie**, another important book that helped me on my path to success.

Read either or both of those two books and you will become motivated to enter the selling profession. My next step was to see if I could get a part time job to hone my skills as a prospective salesperson for when I was free from the military. As providence would have it a salesperson entered our unit one day and asked to speak to the Catering Officer, which was me as the senior ranking NCO there.

This man was selling a book called "The Great Scandinavian Cook Book" which I found very interesting, but I was also carefully watching his approach to 'selling' me very closely. I did buy the book and then went ahead and asked him who he actually worked for. He told me that he worked for himself and was a self-employed agent for a company that sold books door to door. I got the telephone number of the company from him and called them the next day.

When I called the company, I told them who I was and that I was interested in selling their book for them. That I was in the Army but only had a few months to go before I was a civilian and I was looking to sell their book around the Cheshire area, particularly in Chester. I was put through to the sales manager who asked me to meet him the following week and have lunch with him.

I thought that was a nice gesture as he had to travel all the way up from London to meet me, about a 2.5 hr. trip by car. When we met, we seemed to get on very well together and we dined at a small restaurant in Chester near the cathedral. I told him of my background in catering and my idea to sell books. He was quite open and honest with me and told me that door to door selling was quite a difficult career and that I should be aware that at times I would be disappointed with my results.

But then I told him of my plan to approach this challenge in a slightly different way to knocking on doors. I told him I was not very keen on the door to door stuff anyway but that my plan was to approach the many factories and businesses that had industrial catering facilities. There I could sell the book to a captive audience, both the cooks and the workers in the various factory canteens I would approach. He thought that was an excellent idea and then gave me a run-down of the commission structure and the purchasing system for customers.

It all seemed very well organized and before leaving he offered me the position of sales agent and left me with several copies of the Great Scandinavian Cook Book, sales record sheets and receipt books. There I was! My first civilian job and I had not left the military yet. The book cost 15GBP of which I earned 5GBP for every book I sold. It didn't seem like a lot unless you sold a lot of books I thought at the time.

I remember the very first time I went out to sell the books. I had bought a small car so that I could get around, a Volkswagen Beetle with an air cooled rear engine. One similar to what I had in Germany when I was stationed there. So, I knew of the reliability of the car. Piled my books onto the rear seat and off I went on my new enterprise.

I was raw unbridled talent. Reading a book and actual selling are two different things. My first call was to a large industrial engineering company with access only through the reception. The young lady behind her reception desk was quite helpful when I told her why I was there. She told me that the only person I could see about selling my books would be the Catering Manager.

I agreed that he would be the ideal contact for me if she would be so kind as to contact him and ask if he had the time to see me. It's always a good idea to be polite and gentlemanly to receptionists. Fortunately, especially as it was my first selling call ever, he agreed that I could go up to his office to visit him.

The receptionist told me how to get to his office. and very soon I was knocking on his door with a couple of books in my arm, a large brown envelope stuffed with sales forms, receipts and brochures. On entry he invited me to sit down opposite him, he didn't seem to be too friendly, and after I told him why I was there and what I was selling the atmosphere seemed to get even more frigid.

He invited me to show him the book, so I moved behind the desk beside him and placed the book in front of him feeling a little bit nervous and excited at the same time. I opened the book for him and highlighted the gorgeous colored pages depicting the finished product from the recipe on the opposite page. How everything was laid out in order with smaller pictures of the preparation and requirements of the process to completion. He started to show some interest, so I thought I was close to my first sale, so I closed on him! In sales parlance that means I asked for the order.

He looked at me and said "Your new at this aren't you?" I looked back at him and confessed that he was my very first call in an attempt at a new career and that I was still in the Army, based not far from his office and that I was a Seargent and a chef. He smiled and actually seemed to warm to me. congratulating me on my enterprise. He then said "Look, I don't personally need a cook book but I'll let you go to the canteen and speak to the cooks there after lunch about 2 pm. Prior to that you can set up on a table in the corner of the canteen restaurant where everyone comes for lunch break. That way interested people will come and look at your books and you will be able to sell them to a captive audience."

Well, my unfriendly first call had become a significant benefactor in allowing me to set up in the restaurant area. After the interview and with some excitement I sat in my car waiting for the time to pass when I would enter the canteen and set up my stuff. I didn't dare move away from my parking spot because I was close to the canteen entrance which was convenient for me to carry all my stuff in one shot. Drumming my fingers on the steering wheel and continuously glancing at my watch the time seemed to crawl before the 11.30 am target for me to go ahead.

At last, the time got close to the allotted mark of 11.30 and I gathered up all the books I had and the documents I would need for this my first little sales campaign and entered the building. After asking the way from one of the workers I found myself in a very large industrial canteen full of long tables and benches. Making my way to the side of the room I used one of the smaller tables to set up my presentation. I had four books, two of them I laid open so potential customers could see the high quality and layout of the books, and I had my order pad and pen ready.

Not long later, I heard a siren go off which was the signal for the first shift to break and go to lunch. I stood there watching and fidgeting while everyone lined up to be served from the kitchen service area. Many of them glancing at my me with curiosity. Watching the diners and the cooks serving the meals, I knew that that was not what I wanted to do for the rest of my life and that I was going to work hard to make a success of this venture.

Slowly as people finished their lunch some started to visit my little display. I was practically shaking when over the 2 hour period I was there I sold over a dozen books to women and men who found my books enticing. Some of the men had bought them as presents for their wives, one man even joked, "Perhaps this will improve my wife's cooking!"

I had not even approached the cooks yet. After the canteen emptied another siren sounded and the whole process started again. This time I sold seven books. When the canteen emptied of workers, I entered the kitchen and asked for the Head Chef. I told him who I was and my background in the military and he ordered a book from me while we were in his office and then called the other kitchen staff in to see my offer. I sold a further two books making in three in all to the kitchen staff.

In total I had sold 22 books from this one visit and made a prospective commission of £110.00 for a couple of hours work. Understand that this was in 1967 when £110 was a lot of money to obtain from one call, never mind it being my first. I figured if I could do two or three of these a day I would be making some real headway. Of course, in my excitement I didn't take account of the fact that my selling time was constricted to a short period of time when the canteens were actively serving food.

That afternoon I drove around Chester looking at all the industrial estates I could find and noting those that were large enough to offer canteen facilities to their staff. I found several just in the Chester area. I bought a map and found other industrial estates outside of Chester that I planned to visit. Another thing that added to my success was that head chefs would offer suggestions to where I could sell my books, usually places they had worked at before in their own careers.

I even visited Universities, they usually had very large canteens for their students, very few of the students bought my books but I always got one or two sales from the kitchen staff. I was on my way!

The Army's final attempt to get me to sign on for the full 22 years was to promote me to Staff-Seargent. But by this time, I had become excited at my success in selling the books and was committed to my civilian future.

Very soon the time passed, and I reached my demobilization day. Unlike my first day at Buller barracks 15 years earlier, there was no parade or celebration, I said good bye to the staff and fellow soldiers in my unit kitchens. The Commanding officer had called me into his office that morning and wished me good luck for my future. It was all a bit anticlimactic after serving 15 years of your life in the Army.

During the drive to London in my little VW I considered what I was going to do next. I fell into the trap of looking for a salaried position with perhaps a catering company selling food items or catering items, maybe catering equipment. While I was successful at selling books it was a self-defeating item because there were no repeat sales. Repeat sales, I had learned, is where the real money is.

Eventually, I got an appointment with one of the largest food producers in the UK at the time, Joe Lyons & Co. I sat in front of the Sales Director in his big plush office while he questioned me about my background and what I had done plus what were my ambitions etc. I was happy when he asked me when I could start work. I told him that I could start work at any time he needed me, So, the following week on the Monday, I became a J. Lyons & Co employee.

Monday was interesting because I was not the only starter. There were four others who were starting at the same time as me. All of them experienced salespeople. Which left me a little anxious as now I would not just be looking for sales, but I would be competing against professional sales people.

Lessons Learned

My transition from military life to a civilian career in sales was a pivotal moment in my personal and professional journey. It taught me valuable lessons about the importance of proactive learning, targeted marketing, perseverance, relationship building, and the power of resilience in the face of significant life changes.

One of the key insights I gained was the value of investing in my own skill development and knowledge acquisition. By reading books on sales techniques and seeking out part-time work while still in the military, I positioned myself for success in my new career. This proactive approach to learning and growth is essential for anyone embarking on a new path or facing a major life transition.

Another crucial lesson was the importance of finding and targeting specific markets or niches to maximize sales potential. By focusing on industrial canteens and using my background in catering, I was able to connect with a receptive audience and achieve impressive results on my very first sales call. This targeted approach, combined with the support and guidance of individuals like the Catering Manager, underscored the power of building relationships and using the ability of others in achieving success.

Throughout my journey, I also learned the significance of perseverance and adaptability in the face of challenges and uncertainties. From the humorous incident in Grobbendonk to the nervousness of my first sales call, I met various obstacles and surprises along the way. However, by staying flexible, keeping a sense of humor, and staying focused on my goals, I was able to navigate these challenges and continue moving forward.

The emotional impact of my demobilization day after 15 years of service also highlighted the profound nature of major life transitions. It underscored the importance of resilience, self-reflection, and the need to embrace change as an ongoing part of personal and professional growth. By seeking new opportunities with a larger company like Joe Lyons & Co., I showed my willingness to continue learning, adapting, and striving for success in the face of new challenges and competitive environments.

Ultimately, my experiences in this chapter taught me that success in any new endeavor requires a combination of proactive learning, targeted strategies, perseverance, relationship building, and a resilient mindset. These lessons have served me well throughout my career and remain relevant for anyone looking to navigate the complexities and opportunities of professional life.

The Sales Manager stood in front of the five of us and went ahead to give his description of what he wanted from his new sales staff. However, he started from a very unusual viewpoint. He told us that he believed that all salespeople were actually the flotsam and jetson of society. That they were like the leaves floating on top of a river and would either sink or get carried downstream to land on a bank somewhere or slowly dissolve in the water and add to the detritus at the bottom of the river.

Well, after 15 years in the Military and coming across many different trainers and lecturers I was not going to stand for that, BS! So, I at once stood up and said 'Youl'll have to excuse me, but this isn't the sort of sales training I expected so, I'm going to leave now! And I went ahead to make my way to the door.

The Sales Director was quiet for a moment after his comment. Looked at me and said, "Charles just wait there a minute" He followed me, and we both walked through the door. His office was just a few steps away from the conference room, he opened his office door, ushered me through, and told me to sit down. I fully expected him to say "Your fired" or maybe something like "Thanks for turning up today but I'm going to let you go!" He did neither.

Instead, he said. "Congratulations Charles you're the only one that stood up for yourself and showed your metal." I want you to wait here for a few more minutes while I let the others go! That astounded me. The other four were professional salespeople, they had sales experience with other companies, and he was going to let them go! That's crazy what sort of salespeople was he looking for?

While I waited, I had a good look around his office. He had a nice desk, a plush leather chair some family photographs on the window ledge behind the chair and a bookcase which was stacked with books on several shelves on the left while on the right were other shelves behind a glass door with illuminated trophies and cups of all shapes and sizes. I stood up and stepped close to the cabinet to see what the trophies were for and there were 5 for sales competitions of some sort and two for golf competitions'.

The door opened, he walked back in, and we sat down again. "Do you understand what happened in there? He asked me? I looked at him and responded saying "I think so." I said." "So, tell me what do you think happened?" Well, I'm not sure because this is my first venture as a civilian for a job as a salesperson, but I'm not desperate you understand. Perhaps you are looking for someone who had the balls to get up and walk out after your comments.

He laughed. "Pretty close Charles, you see, selling isn't an easy job you tend to get a lot of rejection Although in our business and behind the name of Joe Lyons it is much less than the door knocking and selling books that you did. Still, your experience with the book company and the way you went about it, impressed me, so here's what I'm going to do."

"I'm going to give you a territory which is a prime position for a senior salesman, but I think you can handle it," Then he went on with.."Your biggest problem I think is not going to be selling. No, your biggest problem is going to be where to find parking spaces in the city and the West End so that you can visit your customers!" He wasn't kidding, I discovered.

As well as getting the City and Westminster as my territory I was also supplied with a large rectangular leather case holding samples of tea, packets of powdered soup and Wondermash potato granules. A Ford Cortina car, an open expense account and a salary of £1500 a month. Which in those days was pretty good, especially for a starter like me.

So, after a week of product familiarization and sales training I started my job working in the City and Westminster area of London. At the time I lived in Edmonton, North London so it wasn't too difficult to get into Westminster or the City for me. One of my first calls was the canteen of a movie film company based just off Picadilly Circus. The canteen catered for about 150 people and the Manager was a big lady called Brenda.

Fortunately, or unfortunately, depending upon how you look at it, she took a shine to me and trapped me in the storeroom chasing me about to get close. No amount of refusal or excuses stopped her advances and on my first day I was practically raped. She gave me a decent order afterwards, but it set the arrangement for all future orders from that establishment. It's a good job I was single at the time.

I worked for J. Lyons for just over a year. I was successful in my job as salesman for the London area. In fact, I was leading all the other salespeople in the company until the very last month of the company's financial year. I had a good strong lead right up until the last month when my main competitor, a guy working in Scotland, was so very fortunate. He had a coastal oil drilling platform towed onto his area in Aberdeen and he got the contract for the initial stock for the oil rig. Quite a significant order which pushed me down to second place.

Organon Laboratories and W.T Owbridges

After working for a year with JL I realized that if you can sell it is immaterial what the product is, as long as you believe in it and believe in the company you work for. So, I decided to look for something else outside of food and catering. I responded to an ad for a pharmaceutical company called Organon Laboratories

Organon Laboratories were the inventors of the very first birth control pill (Lindiol 2.5) but during my first interview I discovered that they had bought a famous UK cough syrup company called W.T. Owbridges. They hired me to market and sell the new acquisition's products but first I had to go to the Marketing Insitute of London and take an eight week course which Organon paid for.

After the successful completion of the course and sporting a certificate to enhance my career. I was sent up to Hull, in Yorkshire to the Owbridges factory to learn what they did there, how the product was made and produce a marketing plan to re-establish Owbridges as a market leader. Quite a responsibility for someone who had left the military only a year earlier.

Anyway, Hull was exciting, and I completed my project and returned to the Organon head office ready to implement the plan. Basically, to sell by the pallet load in 14 bottle cartons. where 2 of the bottles being an added profit incentive for the wholesalers i.e. 14 for 12. I had set myself a target in conjunction with Organon's Senior Marketing manager and soon I was out into the world of selling once again.

I burst through my target in the seventh month of selling Owbridges Cough Syrup. Some of my customers were famous brand names like Tesco's and Sainsbury's, I sold to wholesalers up and down the country I was pretty busy and being quite successful When Organon decided to sell out to a much larger pharmaceutical company. Which ended my career in that industry. One thing that always stuck in my mind about Organon was their scientific and pharmaceutical credo "Do no harm." It makes me wonder how many pharma corporations follow a similar credo today?

Rentokill Hygiene Services

I was out of a job for a short while when I approached another well-known UK company called Rentokill. Rentokill is a well-established rodent and insect control company but in this instance, I discovered they had branched out into the Hygiene Market. They now also provide Hygiene services for industrial Toilet and Washroom facilities and in addition they had hygiene services for large and medium sized industrial canteens and restaurants. De-ja- vu, back to the catering industry.

Their service included: Cleaning and servicing all catering equipment and bringing all floors and work areas to a hospital standard of hygiene. The Toilet and washroom service had a similar description of intent. I had to undergo training as my title with them was Hygiene Consultant, a posh name for salesperson.

The training was hard work! I had to rise very early in the weekday mornings about 4.30am when a team of 5 or 6 men would pick me up and we would travel to our place of contract. There we (me included) would be cleaning toilets, sinks, urinals, and the floors and in addition plumbing repairs as needed. Part of the job was also removing graffiti from toilet walls.

Rentokill was my first introduction, as a user, to industrial chemicals. Which I found very interesting and that eventually played a big part in my future. However, for now let's get back to Hygiene. I did this training with the work team for about 6 weeks. One of the stand out contracts I remember was British Steel in Swansea, South Wales. By then I had moved to Barry in South Wales to accommodate my new sales territory.

British Steel was a massive steel producing plant that employed hundreds of people. They had separate toilet facilities in different buildings for men and women. When we worked there the factory was closed for some holiday break which didn't apply to us obviously but made it convenient for us to get to work on the facilities.

It was a giant cleanup job. But here is what my gutter mind found amusing. The men's toilets were full of graffiti, which we had to remove of course. Some of the stuff was quite funny and drawings of the female form were quite prevalent. The poems quite original.

The female toilets were horrendous. I kid you not the graffiti in there was worse than the men's by a factor of 10! I guess having never before in my life been into a female toilet I was not prepared for the surprise. Drawings of male genitalia was prolific and the poems outnumbering the men's in both quantity and quality. I had no idea that women's minds were so much more imaginative and perverse. There's a lesson here somewhere guys!

Came the time when I went to work as a Hygiene Consultant. I did all right selling the services in South Wales, but my mind was stuck on the incredible performance of the chemicals we used. How they cleaned so effectively and quickly how safe and powerful the descalers were. I had to find a company that sold these items.

It took me seven months before, quite by accident, I saw an advert in the local newspaper for sales associates for an American Company called Certified Laboratories. It was just what I was looking for! I at once sent in my application and within the week I received a telephone call inviting me to an interview, to which I eagerly accepted. Then I began to think what I wanted out of this interview.

I had gone through several interviews for positions since I had left the military. Two questions always popped up. "Why do you want to work for us? And, "What are you looking for?" I thought about these two questions very carefully in relation to my future. The sort of income I wanted and what the potential was from this company for advancement. Little did I know then that the two were not exactly compatible.

Certified Laboratories / National Chemsearch

I arrived at the hotel for my interview about 15 minutes before time. That was an old army habit from basic training times. You are either 15 minutes early for an appointment or you are already 15 mins late. On this occasion it worked to my advantage because my interviewer had a 'no show!" so he invited me into the interview room and introduced himself as Derek Corns, regional manager for Certified Labs. After the introductions and the "Put you at ease," niceties were completed, came the inevitable question "What are you looking for?"

I had prepared for this question carefully. I told him about my history and sales successes from when I left the Army but paid particular attention to my time with Rentokill, my introduction to Industrial Chemicals and how impressed I was with their effectiveness.

He took all that in with interest I noticed. I was aware that some applicants would have no experience with chemicals of that kind at all. So, I was hoping that would give me an edge although I had no idea how many people he was looking for.

It wasn't long before he asked me what I was looking for in terms of salary. This is where I presented my "Piece de la Resistance" I told him this. "I do not want a salary or a car I'm actually looking for a commission only position where my ability to make sales will produce at least £3 or £4 thousand a month. Derek sat back at that and looked at me. "Well, Charles you are the first person this week to ask me that and I'm very glad we have met!"

I wasn't quite sure how to take that because in recruiting parlance that could have been a "Walk." A walk is where the interviewer stands up and says "It's been very nice to meet you we'll be in touch." Which of course, never happens. Then Derek said, I've been here a week and everyone that walked through those doors wanted a car, expenses, and a salary.

"This job opportunity Charles is exactly how you described it. A commission only position and the area we're looking at filling is most of South Wales from Barry to Swansea and further up into the Welsh mountains as far as Brecon, Abergavenny and Pontypool. Well, that suited me perfectly because I now lived in Barry, so I was already living in my proposed territory.

From there things happened fast, I bought myself a big 2 liter Ford Zodiac and drove up to the Certified Laboratories Head Office at the Swan Office Center on the outskirts of Birmingham. I Met the Managing Director a guy called Bill Merine, and several other managers. I got kitted out with a big sample bag (again) full of demonstration equipment (hand pump sprayers) and chemicals. A massive book of their products (over 100), a letter of welcome and legal stuff like non-competition clauses etc.

I was now a Certified Laboratories Sales Agent and delighted to get my teeth into this new opportunity that I knew inherently I could conquer. It was Christmas Eve as I left the Swan Office Center in Birmingham to make the journey home to Barry in South Wales. My first selling day was to be January 1st (which I thought was a bit strange as many folk would still be on holiday) but Derek Corns, who interviewed me was now my Manager and Sales Trainer and he was going to meet me at the Bridgend Industrial estate at 9am that morning.

My first call was interesting. There appeared to be no-one working that day, until we came across a pair of legs sticking out from underneath a large transport vehicle. Derek, my manager gestured to me to approach the mechanic and we had planned that I use the Welsh Gaelic term for Happy New Year which is "Blwyddyn Newydd Dda." pronounced "Bloythin Newith Thar" So having lived there a while and picked up a few words myself like "Iechyd da!" pronounced "Yakee Dah" So, thinking I was clever I combined it all and said "Yakee Dah...Bloythin Newith Dah!" The retort I got from the guy under the vehicle was hilarious and totally unexpected. "Fuck off you Welsh bastard and leave me alone!' in a strong Midlands accent. Well, we both fell over laughing and the guy from underneath the transporter rolled out to see what was going on. Derek took over being a Midlander from Stourbridge, and we all started laughing and joking again. Turns out this was his garage and we ended up selling him a 30ltr drum Aquasol general cleaner. My very first order!

Lessons Learned

There's a lot more to talk about my love affair with industrial chemicals but I want to break here to explain to you how much I had learned up to that point in my civilian career. After all these sections,

Lessons Learned *are the essence of this book not necessarily my autobiography, although I do hope you have found it interesting so far.*

When I joined Joe Lyons, I began to realize that it was something of a dead end job. Yes, I was disappointed I had not won the annual cup for top salesperson but living in London far outweighed the scope of my salary to pay for parking, rent, and living expenses. So, I wanted to move somewhere where the cost of living was lower, and life was a little less hectic. South Wales and Rentokill seemed to be the ideal opportunity to kill two birds with one stone. Plus, my salary would jump by an added £500 to £2 000 a month. It was a good move for me at the time.

Here's a valuable tip: *Should you want to become a salesperson and you, like me, migrate from company to company over the years. Always keep your letters of success. If you have charts of targets and actual sales all the better. Build a portfolio in your journey so that when you migrate to another company. You have evidence of success. If you, as I had with Organon Labs, been made redundant due to one reason or another. Get your sales Director to write you a glowing letter of recommendation. Build a portfolio of your sales history. You will find your interviews more in your favor.*

The moral of this is that there are always opportunities that will come into your life. When they do you must be ready to grasp them if they fit into your life plan. What? You don't have a life plan! Think about what you want in your life and write it down. Then think about how you are going to obtain it. Now you have a plan, don't forget to write it down. You can always adjust as you go on.

Likewise, there will always be disappointments in your life but as you can see from my experience it is possible to turn disappointments into opportunities. You should know what you want. If you are not happy with one job, either because you are not making enough money or for some other reason, while your still working, be on the lookout for something that would suit you better.

These days it is a lot easier with the Internet and job searches etc. Take action and find the job that suits you. In the old days working a job could mean a job for life. These days people are much more sophisticated and look for a position that will suit both them and the company. Plus, the job market has changed dramatically. Now there are more jobs available than qualified people to fill them.

Sales has worked for me because I saw that as a way to make money and progress to what I really wanted to achieve. To run my own business and make a lot of money. Sales may not be the answer for you because you have to be thick skinned and learn how to withstand rejection. But if you can do that then go for it. It's one of the fastest ways to achieve your goals.

There are so many new opportunities these days just find one that excites you, learn the ropes and work smart. I have not finished telling you about Certified Laboratories because there is a lot more to this story but there are different lessons to learn so, without further ado lets go on.

CHAPTER 12
LIFE IN THE CHEMICAL INDUSTRY

Selling is a good career choice, and you can make friends of your customers! One of the big advantages of the chemical business is that it's repeatable business. You go back to that customer every one or two months because most of the products end up going down the drain, which means if they like the product they will order again. Then you have the opportunity to sell another product in your range. I had over 100 excellent, proven products to sell. With all those products being repeating items your business grows exponentially.

I refer to it as my business even though it was manufactured and produced in a factory owned by National Chemsearch/Certified Laboratories in West Bromwich, England. Basically, because it was my territory, but in reality, it was NCH/CL business. That was something I wanted to change in the future, but it wasn't to be in South Wales.

Senior management in Birmingham at first thought I was somehow cheating the system because at that time the average order-take per salesperson was about five or six orders per week. From my first week in the business to the end of the month I was averaging 3 per day. How did I do that? I didn't quit! I split my target into two halves.

My goal was to get a minimum of three orders before lunch and perhaps one or two after lunch 5 a day! I'm not saying that I achieved that every day, but I tried hard every day to hit that self-imposed target. Sometimes I got home early because I'd hit my target, sometimes I got home late because I wanted to hit my target and I didn't. Over time I got better and better at it through managing my time and my customer visits.

The great thing about repeatable business is that as your business grows by selling more product plus other products to existing customers you have less time for cold calling. Cold calling (looking for new customers) is the hardest part of selling. But a simple technique I used helped me a lot. That was something called 'Name Dropping"

For instance, I used to sell a product in the Certified Labs inventory called Aquasol. A water based concentrate and very powerful cleaner that had a tremendous effect on oil and dirt even nicotine. In addition, the product had to be diluted with water so, it was a very cost effective product for the buyer, usually the maintenance engineer of the site. With new customers I used to tell them the story how Joe Maintenace at XYZ company used Aquasol to not only clean his machine shop floor but clean their machines also, and at Fram Filters Corp in Llantrisant they used Aquasol to clean the skylights in the roof that were coated with lacquer from the curing ovens they used to produce their filters.

The lacquer was coating the skylights so badly there was very little light passing through them, so they had to use electric lighting during the day. At Fram they wanted me to prove that my product would work and I, of course, wanted to give them a demonstration. I said "Get me up there and I'll prove to you how simple it is to remove all that stuff from the skylights."

They put me on a high lift forklift truck installed with a ramp and in a harness to prevent me falling and raised me up to one of their many skylights. All I had with me was a rag and a spray bottle of diluted (4 parts water to 1 part Aquasol) product. When the ramp stabilized under the roof window, I started spraying. To be honest I had no idea if it would work or not, but I thought if it removes nicotine from pubs and clubs walls it should remove this stuff because they're both a form of lacquer.

Well, the demo was a great success and very impressive. As I sprayed the product on the windows the lacquer just melted away and one wipe of my rag exposed clean and clear windows. I cleaned one window pane and signaled it to be lowered to the ground. The chief engineer said, "We'll definitely have some of that! How about safety will it burn the skin is it flammable"

I showed him the information sheet about the product which confirmed it was very safe to use and then I suggested that whoever uses the product up there should wear safety glasses and rubber gloves because after all it is a degreaser and if you get too much of it on the skin it will irritate. He was happy with that, and I got a 2 X 45 Gallon Drum order out of that little demo. Which came to about £600 and earned me £150 in commission. (From just one order of the day).

So just telling potential customers on that industrial estate about Fram Filters problems and how they use the product now, not just on the skylights but to clean the floors everywhere in the factory and on their machines. Fram Filters became one of my top customers buying at least a dozen different products from my inventory.

How to Approach New Customers.

Your approach to potential new customers is very important. You cannot come over as being arrogant or hostile in any way. So the approach must be very friendly and amiable. When I introduced myself, I always had a surprise novelty in my pocket to hand to the buyer, be it maintenance engineer or buying manager or in some cases even both. We used to call them advertising novelties. I used to buy mine from a wholesaler in Cardiff. They can be anything from decent writing pens, calculators to anything that had value to the purchaser. Sometimes I would buy Marks & Spencer's vouchers at £5.00 each. Those I would buy about £100 worth a month. The novelties and the vouchers solved two different problems.

With a new customer I would give a pen or something similar and my intro was like this. "Hello Mr. Jones, My name is Charles and I'm from Certified Laboratories, we offer a big range of industrial chemicals. We had a conference over the weekend, and everyone was given these nice space pens. They write upside down, under water and never smear, the ink is force fed into the point, so you never have to shake them or tap the ink down like biro's They were developed for the NASA astronauts. They're pretty cool. I managed to grab a few extra, would you like to have one?"

I have never had a refusal! The object of this exercise is this. <u>Should the buyer accept the pen he is bound to listen to you!</u> If a buyer, be it engineer or buying manager, won't listen, you can't sell anything! This simple system helps break the ice and the buyer, if you're not already in his office, will invite you there and get you to sit down, usually in front of him. Sometimes they even offer you a cup of tea!

The pen will either be on his desk or in his pocket. Now you go into amicable phrase. Look around his office notice any personal items like family photographs, honorary certificates' on the walls and comment on them. Ask questions like "is that your family, that's a lovely photograph." Try to relax even tell a joke if you feel that the buyer has a sense of humor. Then lead into your presentation.

The Presentation

First rise from your chair and ask "may I stand beside you so that I can point out the products in my book?" They will probably say "yes" 9 out of 10 times. But, if he says "No just pass me the book!" He's not serious and you're probably wasting your time. Although I have made a few sales when the buyer has taken control because the product range was so big they found something that met a need. If at all possible, NEVER let the product book out of your hands because you lose control of the sale. Now this isn't a sales training book I'm just looking to help those who read this book and think it may be a good idea to get into a sales career, which can be a lucrative business to get into.

My experience with Fram led to me starting my first business. I realized that most if not all maintenance engineers were quite insular. Many had worked for their company for most of their life and their maintenance problems were solely related to the business they worked for. However, my view was quite different, having visited many different companies and manufacturers, generally, they all had similar problems.

So, in a new customer situation I would usually open with something like "You know the problem you have with XXXXX". depending upon which product you are going to sell and how observant you are on your way into the factory.

The National Environmental Reasearch Council

One day I called upon the National Environmental Research Council Dockyards in Barry, South Wales (where I lived at the time). The NERC owned several large research ships and three of them were being redeployed from the Pacific Ocean to the Antarctic Ocean. Their hulls and superstructure were white and black in the Pacific. White superstructure and black hull are not a good idea in the Antarctic with a lot of icebergs and black seas around the ships would be difficult to see. They needed them repainted in orange and green to stand out against the black and white of that environment.

They also needed the job done fast because while two of the ships were in dock at Barry one of the other ships was also arriving soon, and they needed dock space so the manager of the project asked me if I knew anyone who could help them out. I said I could do it! If they bought the paint they needed and the equipment such as rollers and paint brushes etc. I would provide the workforce.

We agreed on a sum for the work and off I went to call some of my friends. I gathered a team of eight men, and we started the job early that Saturday morning. Fortunately, the weather was kind to us and most of us got well suntanned during that endeavor. The only problem I had with that job was the cutting-in of the ships name. None of my inexperienced workers were willing to hang over the side to paint around the RSS Challenger's name so as the leader of this bunch I was the one to take up the brush and bucket.

One of the sailors helped by producing what's known as a bosun's chair which is a 4ft by 2ft plank with ropes knotted through holes at each corner. Each corner rope was spliced into the main rope that lowered me down the side of the ship by the bow. I also had a safety harness on in case I fell. They lowered me down into position then lowered the can of paint together with a paint brush and a roller and pan. I had both port and starboard sides to do so that ended up as my specially for all three ships.

We got the job done on time and both my team and the customer were very happy with the result. The team, especially for the extra cash in their pockets. I did much more business with that organization over time. I then launched a company called Steam Cleaning South Wales Ltd. Although it had very little to do with steam cleaning. The name was derived from a single job, we did for another customer who needed to invoice us, so I had to launch a company in order to produce legitimate invoices and that was how it happened.

I ended up buying a massive, truck loaded with a high-pressure water jet which we used to de-rust and descale ships hatches that had got jammed through rust produced by salt water and spray, we also used it for drain clearance and a singularly special job which was born from my experience with Rentokill. The cleaning of Kitchen equipment.

Bread is Big Business!

Bread is known as a staple food. So, it's big business everywhere. The big bread companies all tend to use very similar equipment, which is a very large rotating oven. The oven doesn't rotate, but the inside of the oven is a chain driven mechanism that rotates dozens of metal plates slowly around the oven.

They use metal bread baking tins, usually four locked together by a metal strap. Thus, the name bread baking straps for these items. On each rotary plate there will be about six or seven of these straps. And the whole thing rotates upwards as they place the straps on each plate. When the plates are full the right temperature is set and the whole thing is set in motion and generally continues all day

After a set time the first of the plates that were filled arrive at the oven mouth again and are removed by the bakers. All nice and brown, cooked to perfection and ready to go, when the bread has cooled, to the slicing equipment. Then they are wrapped and ready for distribution. So now you know how your bread is made. So, what problems do they have?

The straps were the main problem, oil was sprayed into them by a machine as they rolled along a conveyor belt and this system was being used continuously. The straps would cycle like this about 5 or 6 times a day. As the bread was removed from the straps the straps would be re-oiled ready for the prepared dough to be dumped into each tin in the strap, then moved on towards the oven process.

Over time the tins in the straps would get coked with carbon from the continuous oiling, heating and cooling process and after a while each strap had to be made redundant. Therein lay an opportunity for me. I visited the bakery engineer of several bakeries in the South and North Wales area. They all had the same problem, what to do with the accumulating pile of redundant straps.

My suggestion was "What would it be worth to you if I could rejuvenate the straps for you?" I got the business from nearly every big bakers in Wales. I already had the power washer. I rented premises for the job, Bought and set up giant tanks to soak the straps in, one of which had gas fired heating underneath and into which we pored gallons of caustic soda and water that we heated up. We would then carefully lower the straps into the soda and let them cook for about two hours. Then we fished them out, placed them in the cold water tank for a few minutes, removed them from that tank and sprayed them off with our pressure washer, and air dried them. Next, we lightly oiled them with an edible oil and stacked them ready to take back to the bakers.

I always made sure the staff used protective clothing during the loading and unloading of the vats. Caustic Soda is nasty stuff on the skin, and I didn't want any problems in that direction. Besides, the security and well-being of your staff is always paramount in any well run business.

When the straps were returned to the bakeries the engineers were delighted. A few had rusted where the straps joined the baking tins, but the engineers said not to worry about that because when they spray oil on the straps the mist gets everywhere, and it will kill the rust.

We obtained the equivalent of 50 pence per strap (about 63 cents US) for those jobs. Each load was about 1000 straps, we could complete about 4 loads a day so that equated roughly $2500 a day. If we worked overtime because the bakery was in a rush to get them back on-line, we could push in another 2 shifts. On average we were making about 10K to 12K per week. Not bad for a startup business where there was literally none before.

Lessons Learned.

There are always opportunities if you are ready for them. Even now with fast computers and burgeoning Artificial Intelligence. I am 83 years old, I ride a motorbike, write books, and make music. My last three compositions in music have been two for my wife and 1 (a bit tongue in cheek for (President Trump). Point is there are always opportunities out there.

You either work for someone who will give you a high wage or you work for yourself. Let me give you an example outside of my own experience. Before I came to live permanently in America I attended a course in Miami. I was still running my own business, but I wanted to take on a product range that complimented my Industrial chemicals. This product was welding supplies.

During the course I met a person who had jumped ship when he was a merchant sailor and was now a permanent resident in Miami. He was British and noticed, while he was searching for work, that very few house owners in America ever cleaned their windows. Don't ask me why but it's a fact! Back in England everyone cleans their windows or has a tradesman come around every other week offering to do the job.

In the UK, window cleaning is big business. So, he thought, give up looking for a job, get a few clothes and a bucket and knock on some doors. That was just 4 years before I met him, and he told me this story. Now, he has a very big business in Miami, several trucks, a gorgeous office building and dozens of people working for him and not just cleaning house windows. He's branched out into Skyscraper window cleaning, building maintenance and also has a house cleaning business. A merchant sailor who saw the opportunities and got hold of them with both hands.

You can do it! The opportunity to work for yourself is greater now than it's ever been. Sure, A.I. is likely to take many jobs away from workers. But A.I. is also creating new opportunities. Learn about A.I. and what it can do. Ask A.I. how it can help you! Even ask it to find a niche opportunity that you could work on. A.I is here to help you. You only have to learn how to ask it. I promise you it's not difficult at all.

CHAPTER 13
PROMOTION TO SENIOR MANAGER

While I lived in South Wales working my self-employed agency with Certified Laboratories in addition to running Steam Cleaning South Wales Ltd. I was training new agents sent down to me from head office in Birmingham. They were from all over the country. I was training people from Scotland, to the South Coast of England. They were coming to me for training and some to see if they liked the job before making a commitment.

For this I could put any expenses into the company as I usually spent one night taking the new agent and sometimes my wife, out to dinner. There was a marvelous hotel not far from where we lived in Barry, called The Waters Edge. They did the most incredible Steak Dianne with the waiter flaming the dish by your table. It was always very impressive, that was what I always ordered together with a nice bottle of wine.

The trainees must have been impressed because they all went back and told the Chief Executive in Birmingham what a great time they had and that they had learned a lot from my training. Which to be honest, wasn't really training, they were just watching me do my job. Selling my products to customers and seeing how friendly they were and glad to see me.

Eventually the Chief Executive, a guy named Bill Merine, decided to come down to S. Wales himself and see what I was doing. By this time, I was selling 5 orders a day on a regular basis and had a big profitable territory that I had built up from scratch. I was earning commissions of 5k to 7k a month by this time and I was enjoying life.

To cut a long story short Bill Merine came out with me for a week and was duly impressed. Before he left, he told me that he wanted me to consider joining the company as a full time manager. I said I would consider it and, unfortunately, I did! I thought of it as a promotion, not understanding that as I already ran my own business as an agent for the company, becoming a manager was in actual fact a demotion. I would be back to reporting to someone and have other people setting targets for me.

Ambition is a funny thing. And my ambition to be somebody motivated me to accept the position. We had to move to Birmingham, and I was given a roving position which meant I could hire agents anywhere in the country except South Wales, my old territory.

My schedule was pretty tight. I would fly or drive to the new agent's territory usually on a Sunday evening so that I could meet him first thing Monday morning. I would work with the agent until

Thursday afternoon when I would drive home or catch a flight depending on how far away from Birmingham the territory was. Every Friday I was in the Birmingham Office reporting on how many orders I had got for the agent, I ended up with 10 to 15 agents spread all over England and Scotland.

This took a terrible toll on me. We had a young son at the time, and I was rarely home. The nights were spent at expensive hotels and on one of the evenings I was obliged to entertain the agent and his wife. I had an open ended expense account for all of this and a secretary that organized my flights and hotel accommodation and a big flashy car. You might say "Well, that all sounds wonderful" but there were many pitfalls.

Being away from my wife was one. It was hard on her, looking after a baby, and me being away most weeks. We are all human and when a guy and his girlfriend in the next room are enjoying a night of rampant copulation it's hard to get to sleep. Even in the best hotels the walls do not seem thick enough to dampen such sounds.

Back to Sales Agent Again (a real promotion!)

I did this for about three years before I said to myself enough is enough! I discovered that a territory in Birmingham had become available. The previous agent had resigned, finding himself not suitable for the work. Anywhere in Birmingham is a good deal. There are lots of businesses and factories there, so I told my boss I wanted to revert back to agent and take that particular territory.

Although they wanted to keep me as a manager, they had to let me go otherwise I would have resigned, anyway. So, I got what I wanted and started work as an agent in Birmingham. It wasn't long before I was back in the groove again, earning more money than I had been paid as a manager even with the open ended expense account and supplied car.

I built a great business around Birmingham pulling an average of 7K a month in commission. In addition, I was making many good friends of my customers. One day it came to my attention that another company was trying to poach some of my business customers. Discovering who this company was I found that the owner was an ex National Chemsearch agent.

The Birth of Chastom Sales & Service

I contacted him and we had an amicable conversation. He was mostly working in an area called Dudley and West Bromwich, quite an industrial areas just outside of Birmingham. He had left National Chemsearch roughly the same time as I had started as a manager for Certified Laboratories. These are both the same company but under different banners understand. And he was doing quite well.

That got me thinking over where I should be at this stage of my life. Here comes fate again pushing its way into my life. A few weeks later I got a call from someone I had met a few times during management conferences we held at biannual intervals. He wasn't in sales at all but was a chemist. He helped produce most of the chemicals that National Chemsearch and Certified Laboratories sold.

He told me that he was leaving the corporation to set up his own production facility and warehouse in Rugby, Warwickshire, which was not too far away from Birmingham. We got together soon after that phone call and crafted a plan that would help each of us. I was to leave Certified Laboratories altogether, build my business in Birmingham and buy my chemicals from him. Two months later we were up and running.

Finally, I had my own business, "Chastom Sales & Service Ltd." I spent hours on my M.S. XL spreadsheet producing a marketing plan. Inventing product names, creating profit and loss ratios for each product. I was astounded at the profit ratio of the chemicals I had been selling for many years now. Also, I had already ran successful enterprises during my agency days in South Wales with Steam Cleaning South Wales Ltd, which I had sold when I left the territory. I became confident that this venture would be very successful.

What I needed was a small warehouse and office. One of my customers came to the rescue and offered me an office and warehouse space in their factory. A small Machine Stamping factory in Birmingham. They produced thousands upon thousands of saddle-clamps, items used by electricians in fastening cable runs to walls and ceilings etc. They had about one hundred semi-mechanical stamping machines and they supplied customers all over the UK and some overseas.

The owners had become my friends and offered the space to me when I told them what I was going to do. Initially, I was supplying my customers with 30ltr drums (5 gallons) of various chemicals but soon I had customers needing 210ltr drums (45 gallons) of chemicals. Initially I had them delivered directly from the new manufacturing premises in Rugby, but that was inconvenient and added cost for me, so stage two of my business growth was upon me.

I had to spend!

I was doing quite a lot of business with Mercedese Benz Car dealership in Birmingham and remembering my first call there, the manager had said to me while I was selling my chemicals. "We can't do business with you driving in here in a BMW now can we?" I looked at him and smiled and responded saying "Well you had better show me what you have got to offer as an alternative then!"

That day I drove in with an 18 month old BMW and drove out with a brand new Mercedes Estate. And an order for three drums of my new product which I had named "Banisol." That same week I found a mid-sized warehouse and offices in Moseley, Birmingham. I bought a Mercedes van big enough to carry several 45 gallon drums and a forklift truck. I was now running into cash flow problems, so I paid a visit to my bank taking my Excel Spreadsheet and my new Sales Presentation book to bolster my request and obtained working capital to the tune of £50,000

I was on my way. That's how I started my own chemical business, as the business grew, I hired more self-employed agents and spread out throughout the midlands of the UK. Eventually my accountant told me that I had to buy stuff (crazy right), or I would end up paying a lot more in taxes.

The Finca.

Being a business owner gives you some leeway on what you can claim as a business purchase and business expenses.

My first major purchase was a "Finca" in Benissa, in Spain. A Finca is a Spanish farmhouse. Originally, I was looking for a villa but this farmhouse with 2 acres (about the area of a Manhattan city block) of vineyard came on the market and it was an offer I couldn't refuse. The finca itself was high up on the valley's southern edge with no-one overlooking us. The property had a large main room with open stairs leading up to the main bedroom and separate dressing room with a large bathroom leading off.

The whole property was decorated nicely with the bedroom window facing the driveway. At the rear of the house was another building, set alongside the swimming pool, which had two further self-contained luxurious guest bedrooms both with on-suite bathrooms. At the farthest end of the swimming pool was a shelter built Spanish style that had barbeque, stove and cooking equipment in a kitchen area and separated from that was a generous seating area with comfortable sofa's and a table.

Separating the Benissa Valley from the coast was a sizeable mountain. We often took day trips to the other side of the mountain by a very narrow single lane roadway which wound its way around the mountain with many curves, twists and turns. You had to be very careful when you came to a sharp bend in case there was a vehicle coming from the opposite direction. You had to blare your horn in good time as you reached the turn. It was easier on the way back usually at night because you could see the beam of the oncoming vehicles.

After you had negotiated the mountain, it was only a few miles to the town of Moreira where there were nice beaches and shops. Further down the coast there was an excellent marina and bar which allowed anyone access even if you didn't own a boat, which I didn't at the time.

I owned the Finca for about two years, but the problems were twofold. I paid good money for a pool boy who was supposed to check and clean the pool every other week when the property was not being used and I had cleaners in to keep the place spick and span for when we arrived or for when I offered my customers the use of the property.

Unfortunately, on three occasions the pool boy and the cleaners let me down. Not thinking that we would use the property during the winter they didn't bother with the cleaning. We arrived for a couple of weeks over the Christmas period and the property had not been cleaned for at least a couple of months and likewise the pool was unusable to the extent that not only was the water dirty but the pool pump which was housed at the back of the guest bedroom building, was choked up with a dead snake wrapped around the filtration unit. So, they all had to go!

In the end I decided to sell the property due to the fact that it was difficult to find good cleaning staff and a reliable pool maintenance service. One other problem was that some of the customers' I allowed to use the property did not treat it like their own and after I found coffee stains on the off-white bedroom carpet, which was new and the only carpet in the house together with some damage in other areas of the property I decided to put it up for sale.

'Rodway' 47' length overall 15' beam, Seagoing Yacht.

With part of the money I received from the sale of the Spanish property I bought a 47ft motor yacht called "Rodway" (see photo) and also started holding annual parties for my customers to attend at the oldest pub in Europe (which is in Birmingham) We took over the top floor of the premises and I hired comedians and entertainment while they drank their fill and had a nice meal.

Many of my customers were Formula 1 enthusiasts, especially those in the luxury car business so I had the idea, one year, to hire an entertainment suite at Brands Hatch, one of the venues where the formula 1 race was held every year in the UK. That was very popular with my customers, and many appreciated the complimentary hosting and dining facilities right by the track side. I had to spend money, and that I thought was best for growing my business, keeping my customers happy.

Occasionally I invited customers to spend the weekend with me on my yacht and I would take

them on trips from Brixham along the coast to towards Dartmouth and up the River Dart as far as we could go where we would tie up to a buoy (about a mile and a half inland where the river widened into a lake). Then we lowered the tender (a 15' rigid Inflatable, decked out like a speed boat with a steering wheel (helm) in the forward, starboard position and a powerful 2lt outboard motor connected to the helm.

We would take the tender further north where the lake flowed back into the river as far up the river as we could (the tender could seat 6 people comfortably) and when the river became too shallow, we all got out and pushed/carried it about another 100 yds to a magnificent pub called The Malster's Arms, situated on the bank of Harbourne River which runs off the The Dart. There, they had a small

dock where we could drag the tender out of the water and then climb up the wooden stairs to the veranda overlooking the river.

This was a favorite adventure for many of my customers with the excitement of the journey and the delightful view from the pub's veranda to their excellent cuisine and of course the beer, usually for the men and wine for the ladies.

Lessons Learned.

One thing I should explain about the chemical business. First of all, it is very profitable, you're talking in terms of several hundred percentile profit, some over a thousand. Most of the products are further diluted with water. You sell them as concentrates which the customer dilutes for their use, be it for degreasing equipment, or cleaning the oil trodden floors, this one product was my top seller "Banisol", but we had a hundred other products to sell from hand cleaners to descalers for urinals. (Hello Rentokill).

You have no idea how they can get so scaled up in a factory environment. The common denominator of all these products was that nearly all of them ended up down the drain! Which meant resupply about every one or two months. So, my business grew exponentially. Every existing customer would be a new customer for one of my other products nearly every time I visited them, and every product a repeatable product. I timed my calls so that their drums would be nearly empty when I called. That way I nearly always got 5 to 7 orders every day and when I took on my own agents, I taught them my way to sell and to time their calls the same way.

Cold Calling

Cold calling is an important part of a salespersons life. Initially it's the life blood of your business, but as your business grows you have less time for cold calling because you're switching to servicing your existing customers. So, there is only one or perhaps two ways to meet this problem. You either hire another agent to open up new territories for you or you save one or two days a month for purely cold calling.

It is not wise to totally rely on existing business. Things happen that you have no control over. You may lose the business to a competitor. The business may close down. I once lost a business in a most horrible way. I was supplying a product to the local hospital morgue. The mortician was busy and beckoned me into his mortuary workshop where there lay a cadaver he was working on.

When I got closer, I recognized the cadaver on the table and said "Hey that's one of my customers!" 'Not any more he's not!" retorted the mortician.

The guy on the table owned a small factory in Birmingham supplying parts to the British Motor Corporation, He died of a massive heart attack. The moral of this story is your business will always leak some customers for one reason or another. You cannot sit on your haunches saying to yourself this is my business I don't need to do anything more to it.

If a business isn't growing its failing! A business sometimes takes on a life of its own. And, like life there are good times and there are bad times. But the business must always continue to grow, and that is your responsibility as owner of a business. In this book you are learning a lot about the chemical business. But there are life lessons here too. Like taking opportunities when they come your way.

Taking a risk on yourself, I knew nothing about the chemical business until I joined Rentokill so many years ago. Then, after I saw an ad in the local newspaper for chemical company agents, I went for it lock stock and barrel. Another thing to be wary of is getting stuck in a rut! If you are in a dead end job which is leading you nowhere fast. Get out! Find a job you like or start your own business.

But, before you do I suggest you get your head around Microsoft Excel I believe it's the one thing that really helped me put together a proficient cash-flow plan that my bankers would accept. The plans I offered were always underscored by current actual sales, the number of potential new customers and their minimum potential sales for each month. Once you get the hang of XL it's quite easy and you certainly don't need to be a mathematician to use it. It does the math for you!

I tell you this in all truthfulness there is no better paying job than running your own business. You are the one making the decisions. You are the one who gains confidence with every small success of your business. Finally, you are the one who reaps the greatest rewards. There are arguments going on in this country right now about Capitalism and Socialism. The strange thing is that it's many of the elites who have made Billions from Capitalism that are pushing for Socialism.

They would take away your ability to run your own business to ensure that you spend the rest of your life as a wage slave. They have gone so far into the stratosphere of their pampered lifestyles that they have completely forgotten where they started from. Bill Gates for example, the Rothchilds and many other bankers. If this craziness does not end one day in the near future, I predict it will be illegal to own your own business. The government will want to control and own everything. Hopefully that's just a bad dream!

CHAPTER 14
TELECOMS & LEAST COST ROUTING

One Sunday as I sat in my favorite chair reading the local newspaper when I noticed an advertisement for a Telecommunications company called ACC. The ad struck me because I had seen the first challenges to British Telecom's monopoly by the American company AT&T.

Margeret Thatcher, then Prime Minister of the UK, had forced a situation to break apart the British Telecom's monopoly of telecommunications in the country, but she was still not happy with the situation that had only resulted in a comfortable duopoly. Both companies were giants in the industry and the PM wanted more competition in the market which she knew would drive the cost of telephone calls down. At the time a 3 minute call from the UK to America, for example, could cost about £7.00 for businesses and that was very expensive while for ex-pats phoning home it was also annoyingly exorbitant.

So, I looked at that and thought here is fruit ripe for the picking. Monday morning early, I called the number on the advertisement. The appointment I managed to get was based in London a few days later, so I began preparing for what I believed to be a pivotal moment in the UK telecoms industry. I wasn't far wrong. We met in an impressive office complex in South London. The person I spoke to was a regional manager who looked after the different telecoms dealerships around the UK.

He told me what they were doing, which I found extremely interesting. He was looking for telephone sales and installation companies that had an existing customer database to which they could sell, Least Cost Routing facilities, on behalf of his corporation, ACC. He said they had a multi-million (£) pound switch (exchange) based there in London and were about to open another one in Bristol with yet another to follow in Manchester about 12 months later.

The prices to America were incredibly low when compared to BT or AT&T. For example, a 3 minute call to America would be reduced by about 60% and all that was needed to generate this dramatic change was to add a small box to the wall from the main telephone system or at the wall point of every office extension.

There wouldn't be any cost because ACC customer equipment, the small wall boxes, would route all future calls to ACC's central switch in London, bypassing completely the two giant telecoms monopolies. The client company would save very significant costs on all future telephone calls after the equipment was plugged in and working.

The dealerships would make 40% on every call made through those small boxes on the customer's wall. What an opportunity! He had finished talking, now It was my turn to make my presentation to him. I sensed he was already slightly disappointed because he was totally focused on telephone equipment sales companies of which I was not.

I proved that I had a very successful company and a lot of industrial customers. I told him that we and our sales people already worked on a commission only basis but with my customer database alone we could make a very good business for all three entities. ACC the Customer and us. Alas it wasn't to be!

I got walked! For the very first time in my life, I received those mild but dreadful words, to one that knows, Arm around the shoulder, ushering you towards the door and speaking the words "Thanks for coming today, Charles, we'll be in touch!"

All the way, during the drive back to the Midlands I was furious with myself. What had I missed? What could I have said better? I knew why he had rejected my proposal, because he had always seen his project as being closely tied with telecommunication equipment sales. It made sense, they were at the apex of his marketing plan, and he had not considered anything else.

I got home that evening and was upset about having been walked. So, I sat down and looked at it from his point of view and realized that he would think 'How can chemical salespeople sell Least Cost Routing when they mainly speak to maintenance engineers? Engineers!" That's it! I thought I had been approaching this the wrong way. It was too late to contact him again now so. I waited until the following morning, with some difficulty sleeping that night because I was excited by my plan.

The following morning, impatiently waiting for the 9 am general start time (actually I waited until 20 past 9 so that he could get his morning coffee) I called him again. The secretary confirmed he would speak to me as I thought that may have been an obstacle to overcome. "Hello Charles," he said "how can I help you this morning?" I said, "Paul, you have made a terrible mistake, or maybe I did, you didn't give me the chance to give you my full marketing plan." He chuckled and said "go on"

The fact that he was prepared to listen to me was a good sign that at least yesterday he had been impressed with what I had told him. But now I understood the weakness in my earlier presentation. I reiterated a lot of what I had told him the day before, but I added that <u>our experience in hiring commission only salespeople in our market gave us an edge in recruiting new salespeople whose ONLY purpose would be to sell Least Cost Routing!</u>

I would form another company and we would hire new sales personnel just for that company, which would specialize purely in LCR. Finally, I told him I would personally contact my existing industrial customers and approach them for the ACC least cost routing business.

He went for it! He asked me if I would drive down to London again so that he could get us signed up and meet the General Manager. Afterwards, we would have lunch together while we discussed a marketing plan. I was elated! "Of course," I said, I would drive down again the following day.

He responded by saying, 'Park in our office car park again and make your way just across the street from the office, there you'll see a small restaurant, I'll meet you in there about 11.30 am. We'll have a quick discussion before meeting with the MD who will join us for lunch. How's that?" I said "No problem, I'll be there on time." That was the start of a very successful dealership I called "Teleconomy."

Teleconomy.

I went into partnership with a friend called Brian, this was my first partnership. We split our duties like this, I would look after recruiting the salespeople, training and sales and Brian would look after the books, paying commissions and administration of the company in general. It worked out well for 4 years. In that time, we beat all records.

We hired over a hundred salespeople from all over the country. Everyone was excited and highly motivated. Our income was growing every month and once a year we won long weekend trips all over Europe, from ACC's annual dealership competitions for the top five dealers in the country.

Istanbul, Turkey

We all stayed at the Intercontinental Hotel. Brian, myself and our wives. They have a glass semicircular staircase that rises onto the first floor, (Mezzanine). It is so very impressive. The bedrooms were luxurious, their massive bed pillows were the best I have ever slept on, but they flatly refused to sell any to me. We visited the famous mosque the, Hagia Sophia (Aya Sofya) that has four minarets, Inside is like a palace with lots of gold inlaid decorations.

We also visited the famous market nearby called the Grand Bazaar where everything is for sale, but you must haggle to buy anything there otherwise you will end up paying far too much.

Turkey is a very interesting place being surrounded by no less than eight different countries and their shores are encroached by The Aegean Sea to the west, The Mediterranean Sea to the south and the Black Sea to the north. They also have The Sea of Marmara which is an inland sea that connects the Argean Sea and the Black Sea through the Dardanelles and the Bosphorus Straits. We spent our last evening there in a marvelous water-side restaurant, with tables on the open veranda overlooking the Aegean Sea.

Champagne, France.

Champagne was another exciting place to visit (not just for the sparkling bubbles), although we had plenty of opportunity to sample several different types of Champagne. The Champagne production chateau is in the heart of Champagne, of course, but it is very deceiving as to its actual size.

The storage cellars are so vast that you have to travel by an underground railway to get to the different cellars and vintages. Truly an incredible place. We had a lot of fun there. We got to sample so many different champagnes that many of us were a bit tipsy by the time we left the site

During our stay there we had a helicopter arrive near our hotel and I said "Oh look, there's someone with a pot of money arriving at the hotel." The helicopter was actually for us! We were taken up and flew over lakes and magnificent chateau's that looked like something out of a child's fairy tale book. We really enjoyed that long weekend of fun and champagne

Switzerland.

Another year we went to Switzerland. To an area known as the Jungfraujoch. Our hotel is overlooked by the Bernese Alps. The specific mountain is called the "Jungfrau" As crazy as it sounds, on top of that mountain is a restaurant. Access to the mountaintop is by The Jungfrau Railway which rides up higher and higher until it reaches the restaurant near the top. The restaurant is so high you can feel the effect of the thinner air as you walk the short distance from the railway carriage to the restaurant.

We were going to dine there. When we sat down at the tables, all of us were out of breath and grateful for the comfortable chairs. I tell you it's really strange eating in rarefied atmosphere.

The only thing that spoilt the view out of the panoramic windows was the big microwave communication mast only a few yards from the window, that sat on top of the mountain. But when I thought about it, I realized that those towers helped us make a lot of money. So, I looked on admiringly.

We thought that the restaurant would be the high point (pun) of the day, but we were very wrong. After we had finished lunch at 13,642 feet (about 4.16 km) above sea level we left the restaurant expecting to travel down on the train to the ground station again. Imagine our surprise when we actually started ascending again. Another tourist in the train Joked "My God were going to fall off the top!"

The train attendant explained that we were now going to the Glacier. We all detrained and started walking up towards a short tunnel. The walking was difficult, especially if you were a little overweight, as you quickly got out of breath. The trick was to take it slowly and easily and breathe deeply to try and fill your lungs with the rarified air.

When we reached the end of the tunnel what we saw was truly amazing. Hundreds of, ice carvings. of human forms in striking poses, animals, birds, bears, buildings and the train even, all carved out of blue glacier ice. As we walked slowly through the Ice Palace marveling at the sheer beauty and

craftsmanship of the ice carvings we finally came to the end. Which was yet another tunnel, this time rising slowly to a massive platform built at the end of the tunnel and into the side of the mountain overlooking the glacier. Amazingly there were three helicopters standing on the edge of the platforms, their skids tied down in case a gust of wind might blow them off the perch.

We thought, once again, that these were for wealthy passengers until we were beckoned to board one of the copters. Excitedly, we climbed in and once the pilot had ensured we were all buckled in and had headsets on, which doubled as exterior sound dampeners and headphones so that the pilot could talk to us.

The pilot started up the rotors. After an assistant had untied the skids and backed out of the way, we took off. I was fortunate to be sitting next to the pilot and looking down through the window panels by my feet, I had a fine view below of the glacier. Imagine our surprise when the glacier fell away below us, and we were looking at thousands of feet drop below us. It made my toes curl I can tell you.

The helicopter slowly lost altitude until in the distance we saw a large open field. Lowering gently onto the grassy surface we discarded our headsets and with some help and keeping low we got out of the helicopter and made way out of the gate where a large limousine was waiting to take us back to the hotel.

Interlaken, Jungfrau Grand Hotel & Spa is situated on the opposite side of the Aare River which flows between Lake Thun and Lake Brienz and is on either side of the town. A wonderful short vacation for us. But it wasn't finished!

The next morning, we got on a small bus and travelled to the Lutschine River. We drove into a parking lot by a white-water rafting building, and we all looked at each other a little surprised and nervous. None of us were dressed for anything like being on the water. We all entered the building and was greeted by an English speaking attendant, who welcomed us and explained that we had no need to worry because all of us would be supplied with wet suits and wellies (Wellington Boots). So, we got dressed in our loose fitting wet suits and gear and were guided outside.

There we had a good half an hour of instruction. We were to be accompanied by an experienced White-Water Rafter and were instructed what to do if anyone fell overboard. It began to sound a little bit like my Yacht Tender training, but I kept my mouth shut. Eventually we all got into their transporter towing two large Rigid Inflatable Boats (RIB's) on a big trailer and off we went on a 20 minute ride to a small embarking area at the side of the river.

At the time it didn't look very rapid to me. The Helmsmen and staff, with some help from group, managed to get the heavy RIB's to the side of the water while the staff held them close to the side with rope lines. We got in first right at the front of our RIB. There was no helm or outboard on these boats! When everyone was in (the RIB's took about 16 people each plus the helmsman who sat on the rubber ring of the RIB holding the tiller.) We were pushed off, and we drifted downstream following the river's slow current.

We began to hear the roar of the river as we gathered speed going down an incline and we noticed some nasty looking rocks in the distance. All who were seated on the edges of the boat had been given sturdy paddles. And our helmsman started shouting "starboard side row or portside dig" while he used the rudder to guide us past the obstacles. We were now moving a lot faster and many of us were getting wet. But it was a lot of fun!

These yearly vacations were fought for every year by the top dealerships in the UK. We won every single year, as we became the largest dealership of its kind in the United Kingdom.

Lessons Learned

Seize opportunities: When I saw the advertisement for ACC, I recognized the potential in the emerging telecommunications market. Despite not having a background in the industry, I took a chance and pursued the opportunity. This experience taught me the importance of seizing opportunities when they present themselves, even if they lie outside your usual domain. By being open to new possibilities and willing to take calculated risks, you can open doors to exciting ventures and personal growth.

Adapt and persist: My first approach to securing the ACC dealership was met with rejection. Instead of giving up, I took the time to reflect on my strategy, find the weaknesses in my presentation, and adapt accordingly. By revising my plan and persistently reaching out to the manager, I was able to turn a "no" into a "yes." This experience reinforced the value of adaptability and persistence in the face of setbacks. In business and in life, challenges are inevitable. The key is to learn from them, adjust your approach, and keep pushing forward with determination.

Choose the right partners: The success of Teleconomy was greatly influenced by my partnership with Brian. By using our individual strengths – my focus on sales and his attention to administration – we were able to build a thriving business. This experience underscored the importance of selecting partners who complement your skills and share your vision. The right partnership can amplify your efforts, provide support during tough times, and contribute to a more well-rounded and successful venture.

Enjoy the fruits of your labor: The various trips and experiences I enjoyed as a result of Teleconomy's success – from Istanbul to Champagne to Switzerland – were a testament to the rewards that come with hard work and achievement. These experiences taught me the value of setting ambitious goals, putting in the effort to reach them, and taking the time to celebrate and enjoy the fruits of your labor. While the journey of building a business can be challenging, it's important to pause and appreciate the milestones and experiences along the way. These moments of joy and celebration can provide motivation and fuel for future endeavors.

Embrace new challenges: The white-water rafting experience in Switzerland stands out as a metaphor for the importance of stepping out of your comfort zone. Just as I faced the rapids with a mix of nervousness and excitement, in business and in life, we are often confronted with challenges that push us beyond our usual boundaries.

This experience taught me the value of embracing these challenges head-on, trusting in my abilities, and being open to the growth and adventure that lies on the other side. By willingly stepping into uncharted waters, we expand our horizons, build resilience, and discover new abilities within ourselves.

These lessons, drawn from my experience building Teleconomy and the memorable adventures that followed, have been invaluable in shaping my approach to business and life. I hope that by sharing these insights, readers will be inspired to seize opportunities, persevere through challenges, foster strong partnerships, celebrate their achievements, and continually push themselves to grow and evolve. Now, unfortunately we have come to the end of this tome. I hope you have enjoyed our journey together but more I hope you have gained something from the experience.

Carol Wakefield,

Over the years during my civilian life, on several occasions, I visited Leeds either to train a new agent for Certified Laboratories or later to approach industries for my own businesses. Each time I was there I visited Carol who had followed his father's footsteps and become a talented electrician, latterly to become a teacher of electronics at Leeds university.

We kept in contact throughout our separate life journeys and often talked about the antics we got up to during our school years. Carol had never married during all this time, but he had a permanent girlfriend who had lived with him for most of his life.

Nearly 15 years after my move to the United States of America I received a letter from Carol's partner Christine, Carol had contracted pancreatic cancer and his oncologist had told him he had only three to six months to live even though he had been taking various chemicals and drugs in an attempt at a cure.

I was so sad at this news. Carol was always a vibrant, intelligent and active person and we kept in contact all these years. I had invited him and his partner to come and stay with us for a vacation and we would show him some of the amazing sights of Missouri, promising that they would have a wonderful time.

I decided upon this news that I would fly back to England on the earliest flight I could get. A week later, I was knocking on their door at Cross Flats Avenue just off Dewsbury Road after driving in a hired car from Manchester Airport.

Carol's wife opened the door to great surprise after seeing me standing there, while Carol was in bed upstairs, resting. I told her I had got bed-and-breakfast accommodation only about 100yds from where they lived so it wasn't necessary for me to stay with them.

Upon the news that Carol had cancer and had little time left, they had decided to get married as soon as possible. They had had a wonderful wedding, even though it was arranged quickly. Carol owned two houses, one for Betty, his mother, only a few doors down from where he lived. That house was now rented out after Betty had passed some years earlier. The house produced a monthly regular rental income for them. The house they lived in was also wholly owned by Carol and their marriage was expedient because she would keep the properties and income after his death. Soon Carol awoke and hearing voices from downstairs, he made his way into the lounge to where Christine and I were talking. Imagine his surprise when he discovered me in the lounge.

'I can't believe that you have come all the way from America to see me!" he said. "Thank you, Charles. I am so touched by your friendship." He was nearly in tears, and so was I. We talked about our lives, how we were the only two out of our childhood friendships to have made something of ourselves.

We talked about our lives' in Leeds when we were young and what we got up to. We mentioned the friends we had both made and where they were now in their lives. Some had even passed away so young and some had spent time, incarcerated, due to some crime they had committed. We spoke until about midnight when I noticed that Carol was becoming tired so I excused myself by asking them if I could return in the morning, to which the both wholeheartedly agreed.

The next day I was surprised by Carol opening the door to me about 9 am in the morning. He was dressed and ready to go somewhere. Then he asked me. "How would you like to visit Hunslet Moor and the area we lived when we were kids?" I said that would be wonderful and he insisted that he would drive his own car to the area. He looked quite fit that morning and I was surprised at his energy.

Hunslet had changed dramatically, the only thing that had not changed was the pub that I had my very first alcoholic drink in when I was fifteen just before I left for Aldershot. Carol explained all the changes to the moor and Moor Crescent, where I had lived, which no longer existed, replaced by a modern block of apartments.

I spent five happy days with Carol and Christine, before I flew back to the USA. About two months later I received an email from Christine explaining that Carol had passed away quietly in Leeds General Hospital surrounded by friends and distant relations. Christine had been by his side all this time, both of them expressing their love for each other.

A sad time for me losing a lifelong friend whom I had known from my first day at Hunslet Moor School from the age of nine.

E P I L O G U E

I'm now 83 years old and retired. I have lived the last 20 years in the USA, married to a wonderful American Missourian called Patti whom I adore. Also, I am now part of a very large American family. I nearly started work again soon after I arrived here and thought carefully about working on the Mississippi but in the end the family said "Why?" and I agreed that it's time to stop the work and enjoy being retired, enjoy my wonderful family and to discover more of this great country.

I have a map pinned on my office wall of all the places I have visited and now America also looks like a pincushion from all the road trips I have done with my wife Patti and her lovely daughter Megan and husband Jeff (who's a proud Firefighter based in Saint Louis). The road trips were fantastic. Too many towns and famous places to mention but I enjoyed every one of them.

I seem to have had an effect on my American family over the years. My brothers in law David and Michael and their wives Laurie and Leslie have all succumbed to my Malaysian Chicken and Vegetable Curry. Believe it or not they also partake of hot English tea with milk! When I say "Would you like Eccles Cakes or Digestives with that?" They actually understand now what I'm referring to and usually say "Yes!"

They all have become very dear friends as well as relatives, Patti's younger sister, Sugar, who recently helped me prepare a classic English meal for the siblings, is a wonderful person and Sugars partner Howard, has also become a close friend. He's a great hunter and mostly uses a modern Compound Bow in his hunting expeditions.

I want to mention Patti's other daughter and husband, (her first daughter) Tara and Scotty. They live over the border in Illinois. Both are busy teachers and are great people. I love them to bits. Jared, their son is something of a dancer and comedian and is a whiz at computer games. Tara's daughter, Calli has recently promoted me to Great Step Grandfather. While her beautiful 2 year old daughter, whom we look after occasionally, calls me "Poppy." She's not ready for curry or tea yet, but time will tell.

Calli's husband, Dylan, is one hard worker whom I have a tremendous amount of respect for, but I can tell as the generation gap gets wider things change dramatically and real deep conversations with an "old man" are sometimes difficult for both Jared and Dillon (especially now that I'm going deaf!) Hey what! Oh well, such is life!

Last but most important are my readers. I hope you have enjoyed this book, the stories of my life, and the suggestions I offer to help you navigate your own life towards the true north of success. Remember never give up on your dreams, keep your eyes peeled for new opportunities and when they arise, as they will, grab them with both hands and run with them.

I know you've heard this before: JOB means Just Over Broke but here's SUCCESS which means Strategic Use of Commitment and Consistency for Effective Sustainable Success. When I was in the Military and after I left, I never dreamt I would receive the opportunities I have. Be ready, they're out there and they're coming!

Most people think that you need lots of money to start a new business I'm here to tell you that is not the case. What you need is a good idea or a good opportunity that has arisen from some new technology or AI. Use your computer, ask one of the many forms of Chat GPT for help. Try asking for suggestions of markets you may penetrate. AI is a perfect example of what I'm referring to of a new opportunity arising.

If you're not sure of the future career you want to be involved in try asking A.I. for suggestions, focus on what you would like to do. Think of the many different career paths open to you and choose a couple or more. Then design a specific question to Chat GPT around your choice. When you're choosing a career don't inhibit your imagination my telling yourself "Oh I couldn't do that!" You want to be a pilot or a ship's captain you have to start somewhere.

Once you've made your choice ask Chat GPT again how to get started on your career choice. Today with A.I. things are so much easier. A.I. will even write out a CV for you and provide you with the address to send it to.

Bankers and venture capitalists are always looking for new businesses to invest in. Bankers may want some equity, but they'll lend you the money if you produce a good plan. Remember what I said about Excel. I hope it is being taught in every school now. If not, it should be. Excel is probably one of the most powerful tools for business and commerce that has come out of the invention of the computer.

One final word. When you start your business keep in mind your family. It is easy to lose track of your private life when you are absorbed and determined to grow your business. Remember also there are many things to distract you from your purpose. Sometimes it is better to stay at a small bed and breakfast rather than an exclusive hotel. You'll get more sleep and wake up refreshed in the mornings. Ready to build your business.

Whatever you choose to do my friends, I wish you good health, a prosperous and exciting career, and that you are blessed with a wonderful life.

Live well and prosper!
"Go where no man has gone before!"

With due regards to Spock, Kirk and all the rest of the crew of the Starship Enterprise.

Charles H. Thomas

Printed in the United States
by Baker & Taylor Publisher Services